Life

on

the

River

This book is the outcome of an excavation project conducted by Far Western Anthropological Research Group, Inc., to mitigate construction impacts to archaeological site CA-SHA-1043. The research summarized in this volume was required by the Society for California Archaeology, who originally held an easement deed on the land, and the Shasta County Department of Resource Management, who is responsible for implementing cultural resource protection measures set forth by the California Environmental Quality Act. Because human remains were encountered at the site, the Native American Heritage Commission assigned a Wintu tribal member as the Most Likely Descendant for the project, and removal and reinterment of the remains was conducted under her supervision. A detailed data compendium has also been produced for the project and is available to professional archaeologists at the Northeast Information Center, at California State University, Chico.

Life on the River

The Archaeology of an Ancient Native American Culture

William R. Hildebrandt
and Michael J. Darcangelo

Illustrations by Tammara Ekness Norton

Heyday Books

Berkeley, California

Library of Congress Cataloging-in-Publication Data

Hildebrandt, William R.
  Life on the river : the archaeology of an ancient Native American culture / William R. Hildebrandt and Michael J. Darcangelo ; illustrations by Tammara Ekness Norton.
    p. cm.
  Includes bibliographical references.
  ISBN-13: 978-1-59714-086-7 (pbk. : alk. paper)
  1. Kum Bay Xerel Site (Calif.) 2. Wintu Indians—Antiquities. 3. Wintu Indians—History. 4. Wintu Indians—First contact with Europeans. 5. Salvage archaeology—California—Shasta County. 6. Shasta County (Calif.)—Antiquities. 7. Sacramento Valley (Calif.)—Antiquities. I. Darcangelo, Michael J. II. Title.
  E99.W78H53 2007
  979.4'24--dc22

2007032477

Cover Design:
  Rebecca LeGates
Interior Design and Typesetting:
  Heather Baron
Printing and Binding:
  Thomson-Shore, Dexter, MI

Printed in the
United States of America

Orders, inquiries, and correspondence should be addressed to:

Heyday Books
P.O. Box 9145
Berkeley, CA 94709
(510) 549-3564
Fax (510) 549-1889
www.heydaybooks.com

10 9 8 7 6 5 4 3 2 1

~ Contents ~

– List of Tables –

– List of Figures –

Acknowledgments

Many people helped in the successful completion of this project. Trudy Vaughan, a local archaeologist, introduced us to SHA-1043, and made sure that all the players involved understood the significance of this important site. Landowner Dave Abbott provided financial and moral support throughout the excavations. Camping on his land was a great pleasure, and we appreciate the new friendships he made with us and other members of the crew. The field crew worked hard in the blistering summer heat of the northern Sacramento Valley, which sometimes exceeded 110 degrees. These individuals included Jackie Bjorkman, Tim Carpenter, Richard Evans, Leanna Flaherty, Julie Garibaldi, Tod Hildebrandt, Bill Leyva, Max Lion, Brian McEneaney, Ian Patrick, Jeff Rosenthal, Luke Schrader, Bill Stillman, Eve Tegland, Katie Vallaire, and Eric Wohlgemuth. Several volunteers also helped out at the end of the project, including Eric Ritter and his group from Shasta County, Risa Huetter and Alex DeGeorgey from Sonoma County, Greg and Erica Collins from Chico State University, and many of our co-workers from Far Western in Davis.

Jim Nelson, with the help of Erica Collins and Denise Furlong, did a yeoman's job of inventorying, analyzing, and preparing the human remains for reburial. Jim worked closely with the Native American community during all phases of this work and developed new friends and colleagues as a result of his efforts. Strong Native American support came from Kelli Hayward (Most Likely Descendant) and Gene Malone

(Tribal Chair, Toyon-Wintu) who helped develop our field strategies and made sure that the reburial of the human remains was done in an accurate and respectful manner. Our two Wintu monitors, Carol Sinclair and Lori Light, contributed every day during the excavations. We've worked with Carol for many years and have benefited greatly from her knowledge of the local archaeological record. Ester Stevenson and Veronica Graybel helped out as Wintu trainees and provided a refreshing level of enthusiasm for their work. We also thank Loretta Root for her numerous visits to the site over the course of the project.

Jim Nelson and Denise Furlong (human osteology), Eric Wohlgemuth (charred plant remains), Tim Carpenter (faunal remains), Julie Garibaldi and Dave Nicholson (beads), Darren Andolina (general artifact analysis), and Jeff Rosenthal (grave goods analysis) generated most of the data used in this study.

We thank Malcolm Margolin, Gayle Wattawa, and Lisa K. Manwill from Heyday Books for agreeing to publish this work and providing crucial editorial help along the way. We are also indebted to Shelly Davis-King (then president of the Society for California Archaeology) for working on an easement deed associated with the site, and trusting us to do a good job of reporting the results of our research.

Finally, we are especially grateful for the efforts of Tammara Ekness Norton and Heather Baron from Far Western. Tammara was responsible for drawing all of the fine illustrations and conducting an exhaustive search of multiple archives for the historic photographs, while Heather worked closely with Heyday personnel to design and create the final layout of the book.

Chapter I:
Introduction

During the summer of 2005, thirty-six acres along the Sacramento River were subdivided into six residential lots. The land lies in Shasta County, about six miles south of Redding, California, within the original homeland of the Wintu Indians. One of the prime lots contained an archaeological site officially registered as CA-SHA-1043 and subsequently given the Wintu name "Kum Bay Xerel" (Shady Oak Village; Figure 1). After several failed attempts to develop construction plans that could avoid the site, the landowner decided that the project should move forward, but only after an archaeological excavation. The excavations were carried out by the authors of this publication and other members of the Far Western Anthropological Research Group, with help from several Wintu tribal members and professional volunteers from throughout northern California (Figure 2).

Our efforts revealed a rich village deposit, providing a vivid picture of the distant past rarely seen. Most of the findings from the site document Wintu lifeways just before the arrival of Europeans into the area, in the early 1800s, when Wintu populations swelled to over ten thousand in the Upper Sacramento drainage area. Among the many important discoveries made were the remains of prehistoric houses, an earthen lodge, various cooking facilities, and a rich assortment of implements used for hunting, fishing, artistic expression, and processing wild plant foods. Our ability to understand the food preferences of these ancient peoples was further enhanced by the discovery of

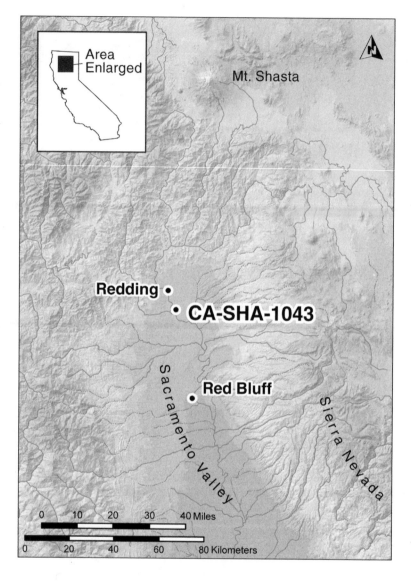

Figure 1. Location Map

butchered animal bones and charred plant remains, the latter of which also improved our knowledge of past ecological conditions in the area, particularly the Sacramento River fishery.

Figure 2. Some of the Excavation Team at CA-SHA-1043

Additionally, a prehistoric cemetery was found on the edge of the village deposit, but it was left alone (as is preferable when encountering human remains) and turned into a conservation area. At the end of the project, however, a mass burial area was discovered in a small portion of the site that could not be avoided by the construction project. Part of this cemetery appeared to be associated with a little-known malaria epidemic that broke out in 1833 when European fur traders visiting from the north carried with them to California a disease that the native populations had no immunities against. Until recently, knowledge of this catastrophe was based solely on a small number of diaries written by people traveling through the area at the time, including John Work of the Hudson Bay Company. This burial site, however, finally provided direct evidence of the historic event, as many of the graves contained European trade goods, including glass beads and a Hudson Bay kettle. These findings provided a clear link between historical accounts and events reflected in the archaeological record.

While archaeologists try to avoid disturbing human burials whenever possible, it was unavoidable in this case. After discussions with Kelli Hayward, a Wintu woman assigned by the Native American Heritage Commission to oversee the project (also known as the Most Likely

Descendant), and the landowner, Dave Abbott, the human remains and associated artifacts from this part of the site were carefully excavated, analyzed on site, and reburied in the conservation area. Although less preferable to leaving the remains untouched, moving the burials did explain a great deal about the turmoil associated with the prehistoric/historic transitional period, including the effects of the malaria epidemic and its social consequences. For instance, skeletal remains showed abundant evidence of interpersonal violence during the period in question. We originally thought that most of the violence occurred after the arrival of Europeans to the region, but further analysis of the findings shows that warfare was a common activity back into prehistoric time.

The spectacular findings from this site, combined with information from other archaeological deposits in the region, have inspired us to write this book. We hope to introduce students, professionals, and the public to the rich, and sometimes tumultuous, development of Wintu culture. Part of this effort focuses on the processes of modern archaeology itself—from the use of various field and analytical methods to interpreting the data, including links between historical archives, linguistics, ethnography, and the archaeological record. The larger goal is to instill a better appreciation of the antiquity and complexity of California's native cultures, and to acknowledge the descendants of these ancient peoples, who still live and work in their communities today.

The book is divided into six chapters. After this introduction, Chapter II, "The Distant Past," provides a brief review of the eight-thousand-year archaeological record from the northern Sacramento River region, setting the stage for the arrival of the Wintu about fifteen hundred years ago. Their presence is easy to see in the archaeological record, which reflects the influx of a huge population bringing with it a sophisticated economy designed to make efficient use of the local salmon fishery. The details of this economy, as well as other aspects of Wintu life, are presented in Chapter III, "Wintu Culture as Known through the Ethnographic Record," in which we review oral histories gathered from knowledgeable elders in the 1930s.

Archaeological findings from the site are provided in Chapter IV, "Archaeology of a Wintu Village, 'Kum Bay Xerel' (CA-SHA-1043)," in which we get a firsthand look at how people lived in the distant past. These findings often correspond to the ethnographic information provided by the Wintu elders, but not always, particularly with regard to the number of violent injuries suffered by men between the ages of twenty and thirty, and how most of the shell bead money and other items of wealth were concentrated in the hands of only a limited number of people in the village. Chapter V, "End of an Era: First Contacts with Europeans," presents historic information on Hudson Bay employee and diarist John Work's visit to northern California in 1832, and compares his observations to evidence found at the historic Wintu cemetery site. This narrative is particularly disturbing due to the catastrophic nature of the malaria epidemic, the lethal effects of which can be seen in the age profiles and burial modes of the individuals that died during this time. Although large numbers of the oldest and youngest members of the society suffered greatly, other age groups (especially teenagers) survived the epidemic in numbers higher than one would surmise from the historic accounts.

Those who survived the epidemic had to deal with a variety of other problems as time moved forward, including the devastating effects of the California gold rush. Nevertheless, multiple generations of Wintu persisted into modern times with much of their cultural traditions intact. We review these developments at the end of the book, in Chapter VI, "Summary and Conclusions," focusing on the Wintu of today and their interest in protecting and learning about the archaeological record. Several positive relationships developed between the archaeologists and members of the Wintu community during this project, and some tribal members were inspired to continue their education through archaeological classes at the local community college. This interest in the archaeological record by Native peoples and other members of the community has grown significantly over the last few years, as evidenced by increasing membership in archaeological societies across the nation. These organizations provide outstanding opportunities to protect, preserve, and interpret our ancient archaeological records, and we hope that this book will further increase the number of people willing to participate in these worthy causes.

Chapter II:
The Distant Past

The history of Native American presence in the Upper Sacramento Valley extends back thousands of years and is characterized by alternating periods of stability and substantial change. Among the cultural groups who left evidence of their presence in the archaeological record of the region are the Wintu, who occupied many sites along the Sacramento River, including the area since named "Kum Bay Xerel," about six miles south of Redding. Wild foods abounded in this region, which included a rich salmon fishery, acorn and pine nut crops, a multitude of seeds and berries, and large game like elk, deer, and bear. But the abundance of these resources did not stay constant over the millennium due both to major periods of drought and to times when population overcrowding may have stressed the food supply. Glimpses of this dynamic history can be seen in a story told to Cora Du Bois in the 1930s by a powerful Wintu shaman named Charles Klutchie about how a godlike figure named Nomlestowa created the world:

> The first Indians appeared near where the hatchery on the Mc-Cloud river now is. Nomlestowa looked down and said: "What kind of people are we going to bring up [i.e., educate]? They need water." So he drew his finger down from Mount Shasta, forming the McCloud river. Then he made fish and deer and all kinds of food. In four or five days all the McCloud valley was full of people. Four different times the world has been destroyed and will be destroyed once more. First there was wind, which

blew the people away; then the water came. The next destruction was by fire; the next was by wind and water; and the last time it was by water. After each destruction a different people came, and each time they were destroyed because the people became tired. The world will be destroyed once more when all the Indians are gone.

This chapter provides a general outline of northern California prehistory, spanning the eight thousand years of cultural change before the arrival of the Wintu about fifteen hundred years ago. Our discussion of Wintu archaeology also includes a history of their language, as linguistic studies have provided important clues about the location of the original Wintu homeland, the timing of their arrival in northern California, and evidence of their westward expansion at the point of European contact, in the early 1800s. First, however, let us begin with an overview of how archaeologists date their discoveries, as that is the foundation for further research.

DATING ARCHAEOLOGICAL SITES

Archaeologists use three basic methods to date sites: radiocarbon dating, obsidian hydration, and cross-dating unique artifact styles.

Radiocarbon Dating

One of the most precise dating techniques available, radiocarbon dating is used by archaeologists and other scientists all over the world. All living things, including plants, animals, and people, contain the natural element carbon. Carbon occurs in three different forms: Carbon-12 and Carbon-13, which are "stable" (i.e., nonradioactive), and Carbon-14, which is "unstable" (radioactive). C-14 is produced when neutrons from the sun's cosmic rays enter the earth's atmosphere and react with nitrogen. Being unstable, C-14 (carbon with fourteen neutrons) decays at a known rate into the stable form C-12 (twelve neutrons). While alive, organisms continue to absorb new C-14 from the sun, which keeps the ratio between C-14 and C-12 within that organism relatively constant. Once the organism dies, however, no new C-14 is absorbed and the C-14 it does have gradually breaks down into C-12, ultimately disappearing completely.

Since the rate of decay from C-14 to C-12 is known, scientists can measure the ratio of C-14 to C-12 in a dead organism to determine how long it has been dead. In the Wintu site Kum Bay Xerel, radiocarbon dating was performed on the wooden structural remains of houses, wood charcoal from cooking fires, and marine shell beads. All of these samples were originally alive and incorporated into the site within a few years after they died. The dates we present in subsequent chapters of this book are expressed as years "BP" (before present), with "present" referring to a standardized date of 1950.

Obsidian Hydration

In prehistoric times, obsidian, or volcanic glass, was a preferred material for making stone tools, as it can be easily flaked into a variety of sharp implements. When a newly flaked surface is exposed to the air, it begins to absorb small amounts of water; the longer the exposure, the more water is absorbed. The water forms a thin surface rind (a "hydration rim"), which is visible under a microscope. The longer the obsidian artifact is exposed to the elements, the thicker the hydration rim becomes. These rims are measured in microns (0.000039 of an inch; Figure 3).

If two obsidian artifacts have significantly different hydration rim thicknesses, we can determine that one is older than the other but we still can't pinpoint their actual ages. To convert hydration rim values into real time, scientists must collect obsidian artifacts from radiocarbon-dated contexts (for example, obsidian arrow points found next to charcoal-filled hearths). Once we have multiple hydration-radiocarbon pairs, it is possible to calculate the actual age of the hydration rims.

Many northern California sites, including Kum Bay Xerel, contain large numbers of obsidian artifacts, made from the flows of the Medicine Lake Highlands, roughly one hundred miles to the northeast. A hydration curve has been constructed for Medicine Lake obsidian using eight radiocarbon-hydration pairs obtained from a variety of Shasta County sites. Based on this curve, we can estimate that 2.0 microns equals about 800 years BP, 4.0 microns about 2600 BP, and 6.0 microns roughly 5200 BP (Figure 4).

Cross-dating Artifact Styles

Archaeologists discovered long ago that the styles of certain artifacts not only change over time but reflect distinct periods of manufacture and popularity within a particular culture. We are all familiar with modern

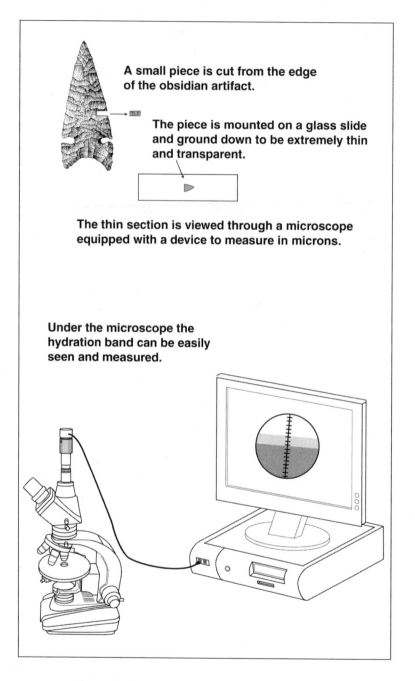

Figure 3. Measuring an Obsidian Hydration Rim

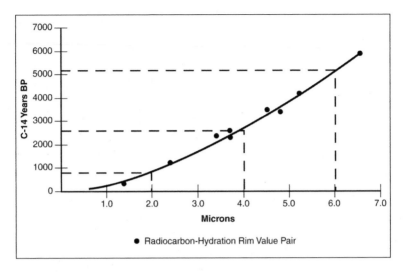

Figure 4. Medicine Lake Obsidian Hydration Curve
Based on Radiocarbon-Hydration Pairs

examples, from beverage containers to automobiles. Artifacts that California archaeologists have found useful for this kind of dating include stone and shell beads, certain types of bone tools and ornaments, and in particular, spear, dart, and arrow points.

At prehistoric archaeological sites throughout California, distinctive styles of projectile points serve as useful markers of a particular time period. Analysis of obsidian hydration rim values on the projectile points themselves, as well as multiple associations with radiocarbon-dated objects, revealed six projectile point types that can be used as reliable temporal indicators in the area (Figure 5). These include the Borax Lake Wide-stemmed (8000–5000 BP), the Squaw Creek Contracting-stemmed (5000–3000 BP), the McKee Uniface (5000–3000 BP), the Clikapudi Corner-notched (4000–1700 BP), the Gunther Barbed (post 1700 BP), and the Desert Side-notched (post 400 BP).

ANCIENT CULTURES OF THE UPPER SACRAMENTO VALLEY AS SEEN THROUGH THE ARCHAEOLOGICAL RECORD

Archaeological studies in Shasta County and the surrounding regions have generated a large body of information from a variety of environmental settings. This information is best organized into a series of cultural patterns, each corresponding to a specific time period. Local archaeologist

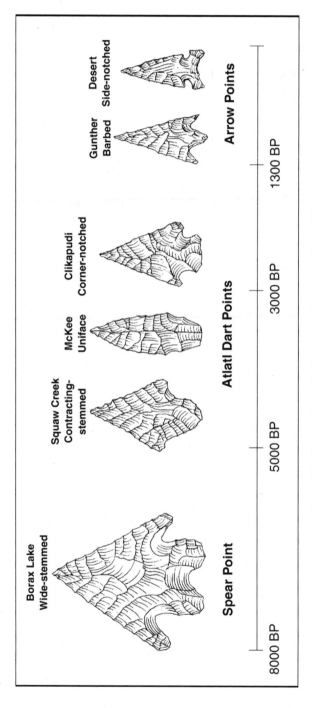

Figure 5. Chronologically Diagnostic Projectile Point Types

Elaine Sundahl defined in the 1990s four cultural patterns for the region: the Borax Lake Pattern (8000–5000 BP), the Squaw Creek Pattern (5000–3000 BP), the Whiskeytown Pattern (4000–1500 BP), and the Shasta Pattern (post 1500 BP), the last of which marks the arrival of the Wintu to the area. The following discussion summarizes what is known about these four periods of northern California prehistory.

Borax Lake Pattern (8000–5000 BP)

The earliest solid evidence of human occupation in the Upper Sacramento Valley largely falls between 8000 and 5000 BP. Most of the artifacts dating to this time are affiliated with the Borax Lake Pattern and include a rather simple assemblage of wide-stemmed spear points for hunting, hand stones and milling slabs used to grind plant foods, flaked-stone scrapers to process hides and other items, and little else. Unfortunately, charred plant foods and butchered animal bone don't preserve well at these ancient Borax Lake Pattern sites, making it difficult to reconstruct the subsistence practices of these people.

Most Borax Lake Pattern sites are quite small and scattered across a wide range of mountain and foothill habitats, leading researchers to believe this was a culture composed of highly mobile, small, family groups. These groups, which probably included a father, mother, and children, as well as grandparents and perhaps a few unmarried uncles or aunts, traveled over vast territories in search of food and other important commodities. They lived a rather solitary existence for much of the year, but large, multifamily gatherings probably occurred from time to time, allowing people to socialize, find marriage partners, and discuss the status of key plant and animal populations in the region.

Modern studies of highly mobile people show that their population numbers tend to remain relatively consistent, often because it is difficult to transport multiple infants and toddlers over large tracts of land, which in turn was an incentive for some form of birth control and/or family planning. This was probably the case for the Borax Lake people, as population densities appear to have been low, allowing family groups to freely move with the seasons to places with available food supply. As a group, they did not rely much on storing resources because the people were moved to the food rather than the food to the people.

This mobile upland adaptation corresponds to a period when the climate was warmer and drier than it is today, known as the "Altithermal."

Studies of fossil pollen grains found in mountain lakes throughout northern California show that oak woodlands moved up from the lowlands, covering high-altitude areas that were formerly covered with conifer forests (largely of Douglas fir). Because the oak woodlands contained a higher density of edible plants and animals than the Douglas fir forest, Borax Lake people were highly attracted to these upland habitats. The low frequency of archaeological sites along the river during this period may also indicate that the warm and dry conditions could not support an adequate salmon fishery, a characteristic that lowered the economic value of the lowlands. Overall, the Borax Lake culture was largely successful, occupying land from Clear Lake up into Oregon, and down the Sierra-Cascade range to Feather River country.

Squaw Creek Pattern (5000–3000 BP)

Several new artifact forms and technologies dating to about five thousand years ago appear to represent the arrival of a new people who pushed the Borax Lake populations out of the Upper Sacramento region. These new items correspond to the Squaw Creek Pattern and include atlatl darts (Squaw Creek and McKee forms) and highly artistic incised stones (Figures 5 and 6). The shift from spears to atlatl and darts probably improved hunting efficiency, as this new technology increased the speed of and distance traveled by the projectile. Unfortunately, after hundreds of years of exposure to acid soil (the product of fallen oak leaves and conifer needles), most of the animal bone in these sites had decomposed, preventing accurate estimates of the prehistoric diet.

Following the earlier trend, Squaw Creek Pattern peoples continued to focus on upland settings, perhaps due to the persistence of Altithermal conditions through most of this period. They differ from the earlier Borax Lake culture in that they lived in larger social groups, probably forming multifamily villages during the winter (rather than just sporadically) and dispersing into smaller, mobile groups during the warm months.

This decrease in mobility and the formation of larger social groups seems to have increased cultural expression and diversity throughout northern California, as several unique cultural groups developed on lands originally occupied by members of only the Borax Lake culture. The best expression of this cultural diversity is the emergence of an amazing art form, the incised stone (Figure 7). Over fifteen hundred pieces of slate etched with a wide range of artistic designs have been discovered at a series of archaeological sites located up the Sacramento River

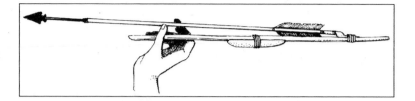

Figure 6. Atlatl and Dart

Canyon from Lakehead to Dunsmuir. This collection, which constitutes the largest portable rock art assemblage ever discovered in North America, includes a variety of design patterns, including crosshatching, chevrons, and in-filled bands; most appear to be abstract art, while others could represent local landscapes.

Detailed study of the form and distribution of the stones by archaeologist Kelly McGuire in the 1990s revealed that they were not found in any special contexts (e.g., at spiritual sites) but were distributed throughout the archaeological deposits much in the same manner as day-to-day tools like broken atlatl darts, knives, and milling slabs. Many of the stones also had perforations or notches, indicating that they were decorative objects worn as pendants by the general population, perhaps serving as symbols of group affiliation and identity. Anthropological studies of modern hunter-gatherers in other parts of the world have shown that this type of symbolic display tends to be most pronounced in places with intense intergroup competition (emphasizing "us versus them"), which may have been the case in the Sacramento River Canyon between 4000 and 3000 BP, when Squaw Creek Pattern people appear to have been competing for land with populations represented by the Whiskeytown Pattern.

Whiskeytown Pattern (4000–1500 BP)

The Whiskeytown Pattern is distinguished from earlier local cultures by a new dart style (the Clikapudi series), the use of bowl mortars and pestles, and the introduction of notched-pebble weights on fishing nets. Bowl mortars and pestles probably signal a more intensified use of acorns as food, and net sinkers likely indicate a greater reliance on fish, perhaps salmon. Although Whiskeytown Pattern sites are found in lowland settings a little more often than in previous periods, the people practiced a settlement system similar to that of the Squaw Creek Pattern: multifamily villages were occupied in winter, but people dispersed

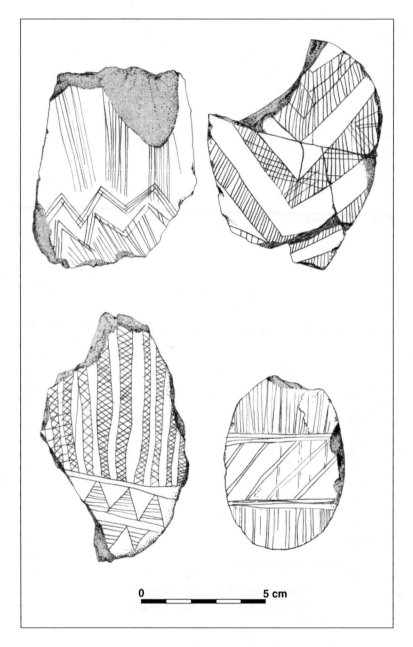

Figure 7. Squaw Creek Pattern (5000–3000 BP)
Incised Stone from the Sacramento River Canyon

into smaller groups during the rest of the year. Why they didn't live more permanently along the Sacramento River and its tributaries remains a mystery to most archaeologists, because climatic conditions became cooler and wetter after 4000 BP, which probably produced a large, viable population of salmon in the local area.

The age and distribution of Whiskeytown Pattern sites in the Sacramento River Canyon is particularly interesting because they overlap with Squaw Creek Pattern sites in the canyon for about one thousand years. Rather than occupying this zone at the same time, however, it seems more likely that the overlap of artifacts reflects the continuous shifting of a territorial boundary along the headwaters of the Sacramento River. The large number of incised stones found in Squaw Creek Pattern sites is consistent with this type of boundary competition, particularly if they represent symbols of group identity.

Shasta Pattern (post 1500 BP)

Everything changed after 1500 BP with the emergence of the Shasta Pattern, which we link to the arrival of the Wintu in northern California. At this time, several large village sites were established along the Sacramento River and its major tributaries, and evidence shows the introduction of an entirely new set of artifacts. The bow and arrow appears for the first time (represented in the archaeological record by the Gunther-barbed and Desert Side-notched points), as do a variety of fishing implements, including composite harpoons and fishhooks made of bone. Large numbers of hopper mortars and pestles reflect the intensive use of acorns, while the artistic and recreational parts of the culture are revealed through items like incised bone and stone pendants, abalone shell pendants, a variety of shell beads, and bone gaming pieces.

The large village sites of the Shasta Pattern contain the remains of house structures, cooking features, and cemetery areas. Dark charcoal-rich midden deposits are also quite common and include freshwater shellfish, butchered mammal bone, and an abundance of fish bone (including salmon), as well as the charred remains of acorns, gray pine nuts, and manzanita berries. These findings clearly show that mobile settlement systems were a thing of the past after 1500 BP, as the local populations settled into permanent villages made possible by large-scale storage of salmon and acorns as well as interregional exchange of other important commodities. Because the Shasta Pattern is directly linked to the local Wintu people, we are able to flesh out the archaeological record with historical accounts from that group (Chapter III).

CHANGES IN PREHISTORIC LAND USE

The changes in settlement patterns can be illustrated on a large geographic scale by analyzing the distribution of the period-specific spear, dart, and arrow point styles across habitat type. Projectile point frequencies were collected from several archaeological sites along the Sacramento River between Red Bluff and Lake Shasta, in the western foothills adjacent to this riverine zone, and in the mountains farther to the west (Figure 8). Analysis showed that Borax Lake wide-stemmed points are predominately found in the mountains, sometimes in the foothills, and never along the river (Figure 9). This same basic distribution holds for the Squaw Creek Pattern, while the Whiskeytown Pattern points show an increase in the use of foothill and riverine settings. Finally, the Shasta Pattern data reveal a radical shift in land-use strategy, with riverine habitats being the predominant location for settlement, followed by foothills and then the mountains, a trend indicating a total reorganization of settlement strategies with the arrival of the Wintu. This shift in settlement is further evidenced by obsidian hydration data collected from many of these same sites (Figure 10). Hydration rims are consistently thickest (and oldest) in the mountains, significantly thinner in the foothills, and thinnest (and most recent) along the river.

The abrupt change in settlement strategy, coupled with the establishment of large permanent villages and the introduction of entirely new artifacts linked to the storage of salmon and acorns, seems to coincide with the arrival of Wintu-speaking people in the local area. This idea is not based solely on the archaeological record but is also supported by the rich linguistic record available from the northern California region.

LINGUISTICS AND THE ARRIVAL OF THE WINTU

Studies of language distributions from throughout the world indicate that Native California had some of the highest linguistic diversity ever recorded. Three hundred and fifty years ago, about ninety languages were being spoken in the area that would become California, and many were concentrated in northernmost parts of the state. These languages can be organized into a series of "stocks" and "families" based on their degree of relatedness, similar to the way we classify the various European

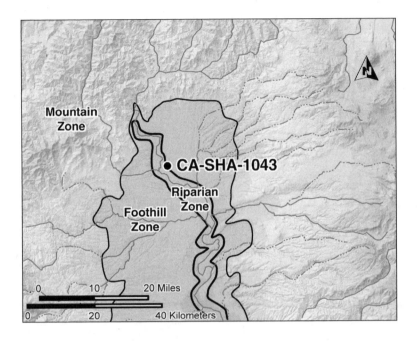

Figure 8. Prehistoric Settlement Zones along the
Upper Sacramento River

languages. When viewing a Native American linguistic map of North
America, it becomes clear that people had been traveling west for thousands of years but were stopped by the Pacific Ocean, resulting in a wide
diversity of populations settling the lands between the coast and the
western slope of the Sierra-Cascade range (Figure 11).

The Wintu language is a member of the Wintun family, which
belongs to the Penutian stock. Other members of the Wintun family
include the Nomlaki, Patwin, and Southern Patwin languages spoken
farther south along the Sacramento Valley and on the northern edge of
San Francisco Bay. Careful study of these languages can tell us a great
deal about the history of their speakers, including how long ago they
arrived in California and, in some cases, where they came from. This
is the case with the Wintu, whose language, when combined with the
archaeological record, indicates that they moved down from Oregon
about fifteen hundred years ago.

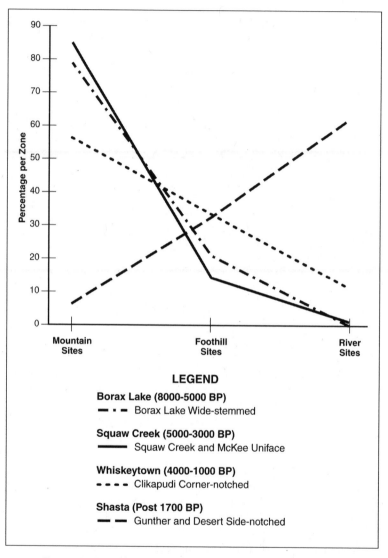

Figure 9. Distribution of Time-sensitive Projectile Points
Across Key Environmental Settings

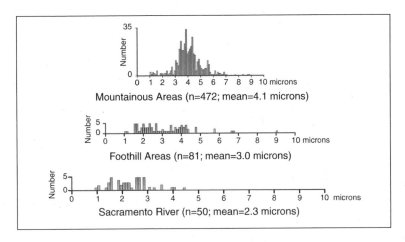

Figure 10. Medicine Lake Obsidian Hydration Data
from Key Environmental Settings

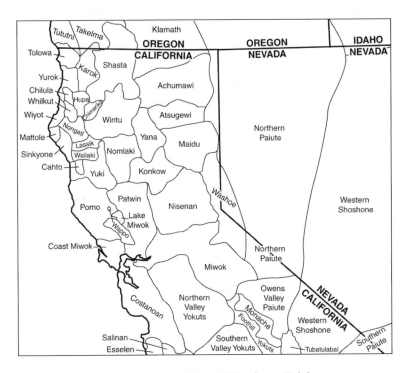

Figure 11. Linguistic Map of Northern California

Historical Linguistics

Much of what we know about historical linguistics comes from the study of Indo-European languages. Unlike the unwritten prehistoric Native languages of California, ancient written texts from Europe and Asia allow linguists to identify archaic mother languages, trace when various daughter languages split off, and then measure how far the daughter languages diverged from one another over time. For example, Italic is a subgroup of Indo-European that was spoken about four thousand years ago. Two branches diverged from this protolanguage, including Latino-Faliscan, which ultimately produced Latin. Spreading over much of southern Europe two thousand years ago with the expansion of the Roman Empire, Latin is the origin of all the Romance languages spoken today, including French, Spanish, Portuguese, Italian, and Romanian.

By measuring the speed at which the Romance languages diverged from one another during the last two thousand years—focusing on changes in the sounds of words (phonetics) and their organization in sentences (grammar)—it is possible to calibrate the rate of linguistic change over time. Putting linguistic change on a timeline, "glotto-chronology" can be used to estimate how long ago related Native California languages diverged from a common protolanguage, even without the record of written text.

Wintu Linguistics

There were two major linguistic stocks within north-central Native California: Hokan and Penutian. Most linguists believe that Hokan languages are the oldest in California, as they have diverged from one another more than any other linguistic group. Speakers of Hokan languages such as Shasta, Yana, and Chimariko flanked the Wintu at historic contact, so we can hypothesize that the ancient ancestors of these groups originally held the lands that were later taken over by the Wintu.

Thanks to the work of contemporary linguists like Harvey Pitkin, Alice Shepherd, Ken Whistler, and their Wintu-speaking consultants Carrie Dixon, Joe Charles, Ellen Silverthorn, and Grace McKibbin (Figure 12), a great deal is known about the Wintu language. The linguists converted the language into written text based on oral interviews with native speakers during the 1950s and 1970s, and even published a complete Wintu dictionary and a book of traditional stories so that the language will be preserved for present and future generations.

Carrie B. Dixon   Joe Charles

Grace McKibbin   Ellen Silverthorn

Figure 12. Important Speakers of the Wintu Language

Ken Whistler's analysis of this information indicates that proto-Wintun split apart sometime between three thousand and twenty-five hundred years ago in Oregon (many hundreds of years before the Romance-language split), while Wintu/Nomlaki became a discrete branch about half a century after that. The Patwin language probably migrated down the Sacramento Valley first and ultimately pushed up against Miwok territory in the Suisun/Carquinez area by about 1500 BP. Wintu/Nomlaki moved south out of Oregon next, settling in the northern valley before dividing into two distinct languages and then spreading up the various tributaries of the Sacramento River. Whistler identified Oregon as the homeland of these languages, as he was able to identify several proto-Wintun words for plants and animals that live in Oregon, but also found that speakers of that ancient language had to borrow words from an existing language in California (Miwok) for species they encountered for the first time in the Sacramento Valley area. Some of the most important plants that the newcomers had no unique words for included California juniper, manzanita, buckeye, interior live oak, and blue oak. In addition to these plant terms, they also borrowed the Miwok word for "condor," a linguistic marker that also helps identify the prehistoric range of this now nearly extinct bird.

Expansion of Wintu populations appears to have been an ongoing process, even into the historic period. According to Cora Du Bois, it appears that the Hayfork Wintu were actively moving down the Trinity River toward Burnt Ranch within the last few hundred years, intruding into what was originally Chimariko territory. Later interviews of local Wintu by linguists showed that they used the Wintu language exclusively, save for a few names of important places, like prominent mountaintops and productive fishing areas, for which they used Chimariko names. Given that Chimariko is an ancient Hokan language and totally different from Wintu (like Chinese to English-speakers), it was easy for Du Bois to identify the discrepancies. Similar linguistic patterns can be found in modern southern California, where it is apparent that English hasn't always been the dominant language, given that most of the important place names are in Spanish—clear indication that a linguistic group existed in the area prior to the arrival of English-speakers.

The estimated arrival of the Wintu fits fairly well with the emergence of the Shasta Pattern at 1500 BP, which marks the radical change in the archaeological record one would expect from the arrival of a new people. An original Oregon homeland is also consistent with the introduction of advanced salmon-fishing technologies and large-scale riverine villages, as both of these phenomena existed in the Northwest before they emerged in California.

Now that we have outlined the prehistoric developments that took place within the Upper Sacramento River region, the next chapter provides a review of the written history of Wintu culture, recorded during the early 1900s.

Archaeological Sequences of the Upper Sacramento Drainage

Borax Lake Pattern (8000–5000 BP)
Large spear points for hunting
Hand stones and milling slabs for plant processing
Small, mobile family groups
Upland settlements
Broad cultural similarities throughout northern California

Squaw Creek Pattern (5000–3000 BP)
Introduction of atlatl and darts for hunting
Continued use of hand stones and milling slabs
Seasonally alternating multifamily villages and small family groups
Upland settlements
Increased territoriality leading to cultural differences
  across northern California
Elaborate artwork

Whiskeytown Pattern (4000–1500 BP)
Continued use of atlatl and darts
Introduction of bowl mortars and pestles
Introduction of fishing net sinkers
Slight increase in the use of riverine settlements
Seasonally alternating multifamily villages and small family groups
High cultural diversity
Boundary issues with neighboring groups

Shasta Pattern (post 1500 BP)
Major changes linked to the arrival of the Wintu
Introduction of the bow and arrow
Use of sophisticated salmon harpoons and fish weirs
Use of hopper mortars and pestles
Proliferation of artistic and recreational items
Several permanent riverine villages
Large, expanding populations

Chapter III:
Wintu Culture as Known through the Ethnographic Record

The purpose of this chapter is to review what is known about traditional Wintu lifeways prior to the arrival of Europeans to the region, in the early 1800s. This information will help us improve our ability to understand the archaeological record, as it links real behavior to the artifacts left behind in the ground. Much of this information comes from ethnological research, which is the study of cultural groups through comparing them with other groups. Ethnology uses data compiled by ethnographers, who study a single group or culture through direct contact.

A great deal of ethnographic research occurred throughout California in the early 1900s with the goal of recording Native languages and cultures before they were replaced by modern American lifeways. The Wintu were visited by several people during this era. C. Hart Merriam worked in the region during the 1920s under the auspices of the Smithsonian Institution and the University of California; the results of his interviews and observations were published in 1957. Cora Du Bois came to the area several years later and produced an outstanding source of information on the Wintu (published in 1935); her work also represents one of the best ethnographies ever produced in California. Margaret Guilford-Kardell and James Dotta later reconstructed the location of more than 230 Wintu villages based on a variety of historical information (published in 1980), and Helen McCarthy provided an outstanding summary of all ethnographic information available on the Wintu as of 1989. It is from these sources that the following material was collected.

The Wintu were originally a large population made up of nine local groups (Figure 13): Nomtipom (Upper Sacramento Valley), Winnemem (McCloud region), Dau-pom (Stillwater), Elpom (Keswick), Klabalpom (French Gulch), Nomsus (Upper Trinity Valley), Norelmuk (Hayfork), Waimuk (upper McCloud River valley), and Dau-nom (Bald Hills), the latter including SHA-1043. Each of these groups was a "tribelet," a term used to describe independent social groups that owned a well-defined territory. Each tribelet was further organized into villages and camps. Villages were the primary social, political, and economic units of the society. Although there is a great deal of debate regarding the size of the Wintu population at the time of European contact, it appears that most tribelets included about one thousand people, making the overall population something close to nine thousand (Figures 14 and 15).

Guilford-Kardell and Dotta identified two Wintu villages near SHA-1043 (Figure 16). One was on the east side of the Sacramento River opposite the mouth of Clear Creek, where an old gravel mine currently exists. According to Norel-putis, a Wintu elder interviewed by Jeremiah Curtin in 1884, it was called "Momdaltopi" ("Point to the West"); the site was probably destroyed by the gravel mining operation. The second village Guilford-Kardell and Dotta found is Nodapomgeril ("Distant South Village"), located about 1.4 kilometers (about nine tenths of a mile) southeast of SHA-1043, where the Sacramento River bends to the south. This site has been linked to SHA-237, which was excavated by Dotta in 1964 prior to being impacted by the construction of Interstate 5. The results of that excavation and findings from other nearby sites are discussed at the end of this book.

Based on the work of Guilford-Kardell and Dotta, it appears that Norel-putis was unaware of the village site at SHA-1043, thus leaving it without an authentic Wintu name. One of the most prominent features of the site is a gigantic valley oak, which shades most of the area and helped protect us researchers from brutal summer heat, often in excess of 110 degrees Fahrenheit; we decided to name the site Kum Bay Xerel, which means "Shady Oak Village" in the Wintu language.

WINTU FOODS

The Wintu, like nearly all Native California groups, did not practice agriculture, making their living entirely by hunting, fishing, and gathering wild foods. Most people lived in the main villages along the river during the winter, eating stored foods such as dried salmon, acorns, and

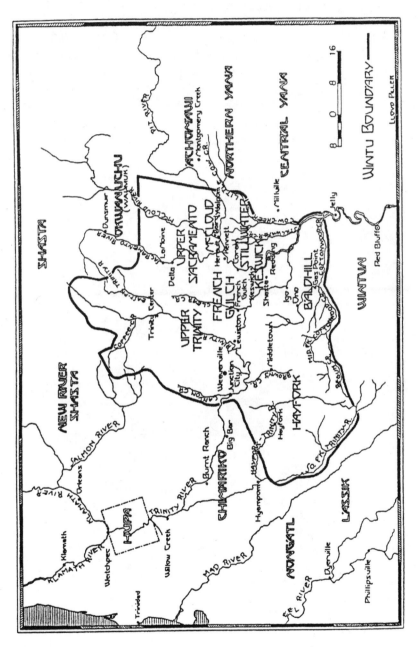

Figure 13. Wintu Subareas from Cora Du Bois

Figure 14. Wintu People from Birth to Middle Age

Figure 15. Wintu Elders

a variety of small seed crops. With the arrival of the spring and summer, some people moved to temporary camps in upland areas where they gathered clover, tubers, berries, and various small seed crops; hunted deer and rabbits; collected grasshoppers; and fished for steelhead and spring salmon. Fall was time to harvest acorns, pine nuts, and winter salmon, and to store them for the long winter ahead.

Deer Hunting

Deer were hunted using a variety of techniques suited to both individual hunters and groups. Individual hunters sometimes wore deer-head decoys when stalking their prey, usually killing them using a bow and arrow. Bows were made from yew wood and reinforced with sinew backing to give them extra power. Arrows were composed of a stone point lashed to a small fore-shaft of hardwood that was inserted and glued into a hollow reed shaft; three bands of feathers were used for fletching. Hunters also caught deer with snares made from woven iris fiber. Placed along game trails, they were sometimes lined with bark tied from one tree to another to keep the deer directed into the trap.

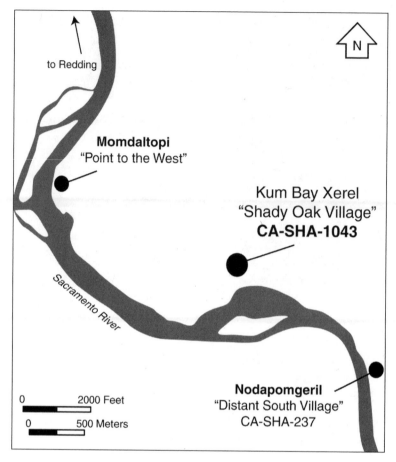

Figure 16. Location of CA-SHA-1043
in Relation to the Sacramento River

During communal drives, one group (and its dogs) would begin at the mouth of a canyon and drive the game up-slope by beating the brush and yelling. Meanwhile, skilled marksmen would hide at the head of the canyon, shooting the animals as they came into range.

Bear Hunting

The Wintu had a reputation for hunting bear, and were even called the "Bear People" by some of their neighbors. Black bears were usually hunted in the fall, when they were fat and sluggish. Typically, three or four men would enter a den at night with a torch and attempt to kill the bear with a spear or bow and arrow while it slept. If the bear woke up and attempted to escape, the hunters would dispatch it as it left the den. The bear would be skinned and quartered and then transported back to the village, where it was cooked and eaten immediately because the meat was considered too greasy for drying. A bear kill was an occasion for great celebration, including the singing of special songs. Bear hides were highly valued; they were considered an outstanding trade item and were sometimes used as burial shrouds for the wealthy.

Grizzly bears, however, were a different story. They were feared much more than black bears, and people would not eat their flesh because they were known to eat humans, making eating a grizzly akin to cannibalism. When they were killed, the hide was removed and the meat left to rot in place. Respect—and fear—for grizzlies can also be seen in various myths about the animals, some stating that spirits of particularly wicked people came back as grizzlies. Many people considered them to be the most evil animal in the world. Young men were taught not to boast about hunting them, as future bears would hear about it and attempt to kill them. There is a story of this happening to a particularly boastful young man from the Bald Hills who was bragging about how he could easily kill a large bear during an upcoming hunt. Despite the warnings of several people, he aggressively pursued a grizzly and was killed; his half-eaten body was found soon thereafter. Upon finding the body, several members of the community tracked down and killed the bear.

Fishing

Chinook (king) salmon ran freely in the Sacramento River during the time the Wintu prospered along its banks. The big spring run began in May and continued until October; the fall run began in October and extended until December. According to Du Bois, the average size of the fish at that time was twenty pounds, although some could reach seventy pounds.

Single fishermen used elaborate composite harpoons to capture fish (Figure 17). The harpoons ranged from ten to twenty feet long and were made of a wooden shaft of fir, two prongs made of hardwood, and two toggles fixed to the ends of the prongs. Each toggle was made of a hollow stick with a deer-bone point stuck in the end and a cord tied around its center; the whole piece was then wrapped in twine and pitch. The cord was attached to the shaft so that when the fish was speared, the toggles

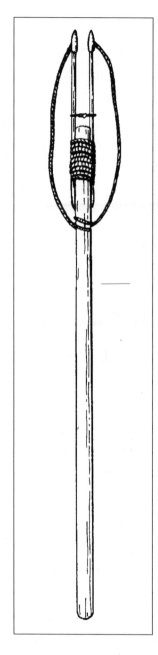

Figure 17. Salmon Harpoon after Du Bois

came free, lodged sideways in the flesh, and remained fastened to the shaft by the cord.

Fish were often harpooned from a "salmon house." Fishermen fashioned the structure by wading out into the water and driving two stakes into the ground forming a cross. Then a series of poles were placed horizontally across the arms of the cross and connected to the shore, leaving a significant space between the poles for access to the water. A conical wicker hut was then built on the horizontal poles, leaving two holes: one at the top to accommodate the long harpoon shaft, and another small opening toward the shore just large enough to fit the head and arms of the fisherman. The fisherman would then lay on the structure, with no light entering his eyes except that coming from the water. Sometimes white rocks were used to line the bottom of the river, increasing his ability to see the fish while the shadowy nature of the salmon house prevented the fish from seeing him (Figure 18).

One popular group technique was the communal fish drive, used during summer when the water was low. With this technique, a net made from wild iris fiber was stretched across the river, and men with torches would drive the fish into the net at night; a dip net could also be used during communal fish drives.

One of the largest community projects was the construction of a fish weir. Although no actual Wintu weirs have been described or drawn, we know they built them, and it seems likely that they were similar to those constructed by their Nomlaki neighbors to the south. The Nomlaki

Figure 18. Wintu Salmon House

pounded large posts (six to eight inches in diameter) into the bottom of the river with stones. Smaller stringers were lashed crosswise with grapevine, and willows were then woven into the structure at one-inch intervals, stopping the fish from moving upstream. Three pens (woven onshore) were attached behind gates left in the weir; platforms were often built on top of the pens to facilitate netting and spearing fish caught in the pens. Some gates were always left open to allow a portion of the fish to move up into adjacent territories, thereby avoiding hostilities with neighbors (Figure 19).

Spring salmon were not dried when caught because they were considered to be too greasy. Instead, the fish were laid in a pit lined with hot rocks and covered with additional preheated stones. They were eaten after cooking, and any remaining meat was boned and flaked. The flaked flesh was then dried and pulverized into salmon flour, which could be stored over the winter. It was also sometimes mixed with dried roe and pine nuts, and was considered a valuable trade commodity by adjacent groups lacking access to large fish runs.

Salmon caught later in the year were less oily and more conducive to drying. Split open and affixed to a long pole with twigs, many fish

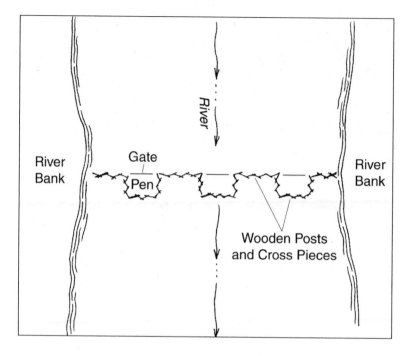

Figure 19. Wintu Fish Weir

could be dried in the sun on a single pole (Figure 20). Once dried, they were folded (head to tail and flank to flank) and stored for the winter.

Plant Gathering and Processing

Many types of plant foods were used by the Wintu. Du Bois provides a comprehensive listing, including six kinds of acorns, buckeye, manzanita berries, Indian potatoes, wild onions, various wild berries and grapes, wild sunflower seeds, many grass seeds, and both sugar and gray pine nuts. We will focus on the processing of manzanita, buckeye, and acorns.

Manzanita berries were processed in two main ways. During hot summer months the Wintu made a sweet juice by mashing the fresh berries and soaking them in cold water. Later in the year, when the berries were dry and floury, they were pounded and the nuts were removed using a winnowing basket. The flour was mixed with water and cooked, resulting in a sweet, nourishing porridge.

Buckeye was gathered in the fall, when the balls (fruit) were fully

Figure 20. Salmon Drying on the River Bar

developed and ready to burst. The balls were roasted in a pit, and the meat was squeezed into a large basket and mashed using the feet. When it became creamy, it was placed in a sand pit and rinsed with water to leach out the toxins. This took about one day, and the resulting product was made into a soup. Sometimes unprocessed buckeye was stored in outdoor pits with good drainage, to be used in spring after it was passively leached by the winter rains.

Finally, acorns were a major food for the Wintu. When acorns began ripening in the fall, family groups visited the groves for the harvest. Acorns remaining on the trees were preferred over those on the ground, so men would climb the trees and shake off the crop. The unshelled acorns were carried back to the village, where they were processed for immediate consumption or stored for later use. Acorns were stored in the shell and placed in bark-lined pits. Those to be eaten immediately were cracked, shelled, and pounded using a stone pestle and a hopper (basketry) mortar. Different from stone bowls or bedrock mortars used in other parts of California, hopper mortars consisted of a bottomless basket placed on a flat stone; the acorns were pounded on the stone and the meal was confined by the basket (Figure 21). Once the acorn meal was produced, it had to be leached of its toxic tannic acids. This was accomplished by placing the meal in a sand pit and pouring water through it for several hours.

The leached meal could then be mixed with water and boiled into a thick soup using a basket and hot rocks. Acorn bread was also made by heating a rock-lined pit, covering the rocks with maple leaves, and placing the dough on the leaves. The dough was then covered with more leaves, hot rocks, and earth, and an additional fire was usually built on top. After baking overnight, an acorn loaf with a rich, oily consistency was ready. The bread could keep for months if needed, however it was typical for the Wintu to bake every week or two.

WINTU SOCIAL ORGANIZATION

Unlike many hunter-gatherer groups, which often have egalitarian social organization, the Wintu were socially stratified, with both rich and poor people living within each tribelet. Items of wealth were clearly recognized, and bows and arrows, elk-skin armor, clamshell disk bead money (Figure 22), and the skins of animals like bear and otters were considered valuable by almost all of the people interviewed by Du Bois. Clam disk money probably originated in Bodega and Tomales Bays, and was considered men's currency (women typically traded in basketry). The value of certain objects was measured using clam disk beads: large fishing nets were 1,000 beads, elk hides 800 beads, large storage baskets 150 beads, bow and arrows 50 beads, and deer hides 20 beads.

Wintu Chiefs

Each tribelet had a chief or headman who lived in one of the largest villages. The chiefs tended to be the wealthiest people in the community, and this prosperity was manifested by their having many wives, along with numerous strings of bead money, elk-skin armor, and other items listed above. This role was usually passed down from father to son, unless the son lacked the skills necessary for the job, in which case some other male relative would be given the position. The duties of the chief were many, including settling disputes, organizing large gatherings, and waging war. He was expected to be democratic and dignified, to have the ability to talk to everybody, and to speak well at large gatherings.

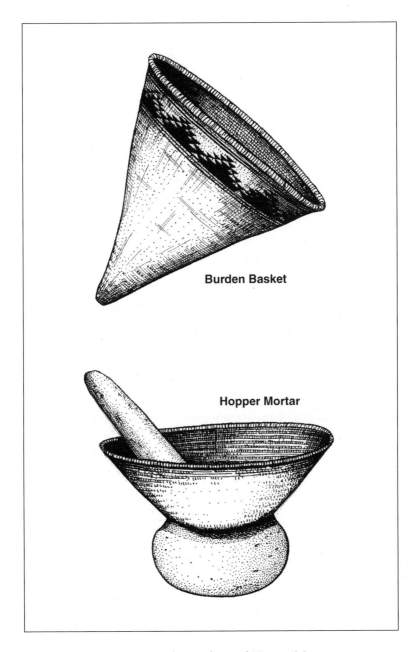

Burden Basket

Hopper Mortar

Figure 21. Burden Basket and Hopper Mortar

Disputes among members of the group often stemmed from criminal behavior. Murder sometimes demanded blood revenge, but the chief could often negotiate a payment to the grieving family and avoid capital punishment. Problems stemming from thievery could often be solved by returning the stolen item, but the chief was ultimately responsible for assigning a price for the unsanctioned behavior of the guilty party. Finally, habitual troublemakers could be, with the authorization of the chief, soundly beaten by the group. On rare occasions, people were killed if they refused to change their behavior.

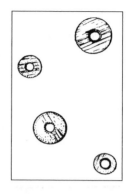

Figure 22. Clamshell Disk Money

Another of the chief's duties was to organize large dances and other social gatherings, an important part of Wintu life. Before a big event, runners were sent to outlying villages to invite the guests and tell them what to bring. The events were often organized around times of food surpluses, like big pine nut harvests and salmon runs. Some people had to travel as many as two days to reach a celebration, and each community did its best to bring plenty of food and a variety of trade goods, both being measures of prestige. Sometimes two to three hundred people would come to these "Big Times," where the feasting, dancing, and gambling would last from three to five days. Gambling contests were a popular activity, with fortunes of shell money and other valuables changing hands on a regular basis.

Shamans

Shamanic doctors were also important members of the social group, and the position was open to both men and women. Initiation ceremonies took place in an earthen lodge, where the initiates would dance through the night until they received the supernatural spiritual power. Every shaman was expected to be a good singer and possess several doctoring songs linked to his or her special spirits. Doctoring often began with the smoking of wild tobacco to help bring on the spirit helper through a trance, after which the sickness was usually sucked out of the body. Equally important to doctoring was shamanistic prophesy, which also took place during a tobacco-induced trance. Prophesies covered a wide range of subjects, including predictions about the location of game and the success of hunting trips, the future health of certain individuals, and upcoming weather. Although intended to cure and heal, some shamans were known to have "poisoned," sending sickness to their rivals and enemies.

Marriage

Intervillage gatherings also served as places to meet potential husbands and wives, especially for people from smaller outlying villages. Although there was no formal bride price, sometimes gifts like shell beads, baskets, or deer hides were exchanged between families when a match was made.

As long as a man and woman were living together they were expected to be faithful to one another. Divorce was easy and occurred relatively often, as incompatibility and adultery were sufficient grounds for separation. Monogamy was customary but polygamy was permitted, particularly among rich men. Wealthy chiefs could have between two and twelve wives, a factor that helped increase their standing because the women produced food surpluses that could be used as commodities for exchange. Sisters or other related women often formed the multi-wife households.

Post-marriage residence could be either patrilocal or matrilocal (in the village of the husband's or wife's family), but newlyweds were encouraged to establish their own individual households. A mother-in-law taboo was in force, stipulating that a man was not permitted to deal directly with his wife's mother; he was expected to keep his distance and treat her with a great deal of respect. If these restrictions were violated, it was said that the man was liable to be torn apart by a grizzly bear.

Gambling

Gambling was one way for men to demonstrate their skills and build prestige. Because the cultural code of honor required winners to continue playing as long as other people were willing to bet, games often went on for long periods of time. The *bohemtcus* ("big wood") hand game was quite popular. Played between two competing teams, it centered around a single stick or bone that was about three inches long and served as the ace. The dealer rolled the ace around in a bundle of grass and thin rods that were about one foot long, concealing it from his competitors. To distract his opponents, the dealer would sing loudly and gesture wildly, and then subtly grab the ace, hold his clenched fists out, and hope the competing team could not guess which hand held it. If the opponents guessed correctly, they would "get the deal," meaning it was their turn to hide the ace.

A team could score only when it had the deal, getting one point each time the opposing team guessed incorrectly. Score was kept with twenty stick counters, which were placed between the two teams. The game did not end until one team had secured all the counters in the center pile and those obtained by the opponents; it could sometimes take a day or two to complete a game. Although the teams had a limited number of players, large crowds gathered at the event to place bets on their favorite teams and join in on the singing and haranguing.

Warfare

Although the Wintu usually had friendly relationships with outsiders and other tribelets within their territory, they did have traditional enemies who were viewed with caution. The Bald Hills people, for example, did not like the Nomsus ("West People"), who were probably Athapaskan speakers from the uplands like the Lassik or Nongatl. They also had boundary issues with the Noze (Yana) who occupied the hills to the east, and many of the Wintu groups referred to them as enemies and strangers.

When intergroup conflicts did arise, they were often solved through negotiations between the chiefs of the groups or the individuals involved. But when negotiations failed and intergroup violence erupted, chiefs would organize tribesmen to fight although not necessarily lead them into battle. The battles were usually small in scale and caused by local problems such as the murder of a relative or the theft of women by neighboring peoples. One such story comes from the Bald Hills people: After some Nomsus came down from the hills and killed a husband, wife, and child, friends of the family set out for revenge found the perpetrators in a hunting camp. Waiting until the Nomsus fell asleep, the Wintu speared their leader and then killed the others, perhaps twelve in all.

VILLAGE ARCHITECTURE:
IMPLICATIONS FOR THE ARCHAEOLOGICAL RECORD

Wintu village sizes probably ranged from twenty to one hundred and fifty men, women, and children, and included between five and fifty bark houses. These dwellings were made from a conically shaped frame of wood, using three or four main vertical poles, and smaller stringers lashed together. The house pits were excavated one to three feet into the ground, and the back dirt was banked up around the perimeter to form a raised footing. Bark and evergreen boughs were used to cover the structures, which were about nine feet (three meters) in diameter, typically housing three to seven family members.

Some of the larger villages also had an earthen lodge. Large, circular, semi-subterranean structures measuring fifteen to twenty feet in diameter, the lodges served as gathering places for the men, who would enter through a hole in the roof, climbing down notches cut into its center pole, or by using a separate wooden ladder lashed together with grapevines. The pits for the lodges were deeper than those for standard houses, often reaching shoulder depth. Rafters radiated out from the center post every three or four feet, while pickets were lashed at right angles to the rafters every one to two feet. The roof was covered with a mixture of bark, brush, and earth.

Cemeteries were usually located about three hundred feet from the dwellings, with relatives buried close to one another. Elders who remembered where previous people had been interred were in charge of choosing locations for subsequent graves. Bodies were buried in crouching positions with their elbows inside their knees, and the corpse was tightly wrapped with deer sinew or rope.

Grave pits were usually four feet deep, and sometimes lined with rocks and bark. Personal items like bows and arrows, beads, or feathers were often interred with bodies. Once a body and its associated items were placed in the grave pit, it was covered with bark, stones, and soil.

Discussion

We are now ready to move from the ethnographic record of the Wintu to the materials actually discovered from the archaeological site. As we make this transition, however, we will not stray too far from the ethnographic accounts, because the archaeological findings represent only a small fraction of Wintu life. Most archaeological materials are fragmentary, like small pieces from a composite harpoon or the burned down remains of a house, so the ethnographic record accounts help us better understand the original condition and function of these items. There are other cases where archaeological discoveries teach things we never

Chapter IV:
Archaeology of a Wintu Village,
"Kum Bay Xerel" (CA-SHA-1043)

Archaeological site SHA-1043 lies on the north side of the Sacramento River along a relatively short stretch where it flows from west to east rather than its normal north-south orientation. The site is located on a small knoll about 250 meters (820 feet) from the original channel of the river and is in easy reach of multiple vegetation communities, including riparian forest, blue oak/gray pine forest, and valley oak savanna. The deposit is composed of a rich, dark "midden," a term used for soils that have been altered by people through the addition of charcoal, butchered and cooked animal bone, shellfish, and other organic remains, as well as artifacts, tool-manufacturing debris, and the remains of cooking hearths and other domestic features. The site measures approximately 110 by 40 meters (360 by 130 feet), following the configuration of the knoll. A large majestic valley oak, for which the site was named, shades its eastern side, and probably existed when the village was occupied 175 years ago.

We begin this chapter with the methods used to excavate the site, paying special attention to the different techniques required to collect the full range of archaeological materials in the deposit. Our findings from the village are then described, beginning with the house structures and other domestic features, followed by a discussion of uncovered artifacts and food remains. This information provides us with an outstanding view of Wintu life prior to the arrival of the European fur trappers from the north, in the early 1800s.

Field Methods

Fieldwork began with the establishment of a one-by-one-meter grid system so that the location of all findings could be carefully mapped. The grid was set up at 15 degrees east of north because it lined up with the orientation of the site better than "true" or magnetic north. We then excavated five backhoe trenches across the site (Figure 23). The purpose of this work was to expose the depth of the deposit and to identify any major cultural features like cooking hearths or houses. This effort discovered several small, ash-filled cooking features and the remains of a burned house. Based on these findings, several excavation units were hand dug to sample the house, the multiple hearth features, and associated midden deposits; each unit was labeled according to its location on the grid. They were excavated in 10-centimeter levels, and the sediments were screened through a combination of 1/4- and 1/8-inch mesh (Figures 24, 25, and 26).

All cultural material was collected from these units with the exception of shellfish, the fragments of which take too much time to recover through hand excavation. Shellfish remains are instead collected from column samples, which are taken from an exposed profile (e.g., the wall of an excavation unit or a backhoe trench) in sections measuring twenty centimeters long by twenty centimeters wide by ten centimeters deep. Six column samples were collected from SHA-1043, most cutting through ash features. Each sample was then put through 1/4-, 1/8-, and 1/16-inch screens to obtain fine-grained samples of fish bone and shellfish.

Another method for isolating cultural artifacts—"flotation"—was also used at the site. Twelve samples, each composed of four liters of soil, were taken from key locations and, rather than being passed through a screen, were agitated in water to allow charred plant food remains to float upward to be collected and analyzed. Information gathered from both column and flotation samples help us reconstruct diets of the people who lived at the site.

We used this multifaceted approach to sampling the site because a single collection method cannot efficiently obtain the full range of materials present in the deposit. Column and flotation samples do an excellent job of isolating microconstituents like charred plant remains and small fragments of fish bone, but the work is very slow and prevents us from excavating volumes necessary to achieve a good sample of larger materials. While the 1/4-inch screens are useful in finding most

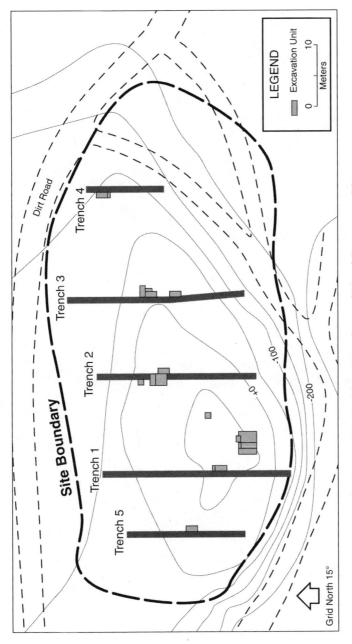

Figure 23. Backhoe Trenches and Hand Excavation Units within the Village Portions of CA-SHA-1043

Figure 24. Field Workers Excavating at CA-SHA-1043

Figure 25. Wintu Trainees Screening,
Ester Stevenson and Veronica Graybel

Figure 26. Wintu Representatives Observing Materials at Field Lab,
Kelli Hayward, Linda Malone, and Lori Light

flaked and ground stone tools, a pass with 1/8-inch screens is needed to
uncover smaller tool fragments, various types of animal bone, and shell
beads. On the other end of the spectrum, use of the backhoe, the most
coarse-grained technique, is the best way to discover houses and other
large features, which typically contain the most useful information.

Once we obtained adequate column and flotation samples from the
features and midden deposits, we initiated a scraping phase to identify
additional features. The front loader on the backhoe was pulled back-
ward across the site between the original trenches, removing approximately ten centimeters of deposit with each pass. This work led to the
discovery of additional cooking features, the remains of a house, a burned
earthen lodge, and two small cemetery areas—one prehistoric, the other
including Wintu who probably died in the 1830s. The prehistoric cemetery was left intact and turned into a conservation area, but the other
area was in the unavoidable path of construction; human remains from
that later cemetery were carefully removed, studied on site, and then
reburied within the conservation area under the direction of the Native
Americans overseeing the work.

SITE STRUCTURE AND CHRONOLOGY

We now turn our attention to the structural characteristics of the site, in an attempt to pinpoint the times during which it was occupied. A site's "structure" reveals how and when a particular area was used by its inhabitants. In order to place archaeological evidence on a timeline, we look to the system of naturally formed stratigraphic layers that might exist in a deposit and/or the cultural features created by the inhabitants that can be radiocarbon dated. We begin our study by describing the stratigraphic profiles exposed during our excavations, followed by a review of the house, earthen lodge, and some of the cooking features we uncovered. We then date these elements using radiocarbon and obsidian hydration methods, as well as associating our finds with period-specific projectile points also found at the site.

Stratigraphic Profiles

The archaeological deposit at SHA-1043 ranges between 100 and 150 centimeters in depth. The depth of the midden was easy to determine because it was deposited on top of an old river terrace that geological evidence suggests was probably formed during the last ice age, long before the Upper Sacramento Valley was occupied by people. The terrace includes a high density of boulders, cobbles, and gravels mixed together with yellowish-brown sands that form a stark contrast with the dark grayish-brown midden. Even though the midden sits on this old surface and is rather thick, it represents less than one thousand years of occupation.

A soil profile from a SHA-1043 excavation unit, S7/W23, illustrates the stratigraphic relationships exposed at the site (Figure 27). Most of the deposit is a very dark brown (almost black) rocky, sandy loam. Much of the rock is burned and fractured, representing the remains of hearths, earth ovens, salmon roasting features, or stones used to heat meals in cooking baskets. Little flecks of white mussel shell can be seen throughout the deposit, while larger concentrations of shell occur here and there, occasionally associated with high densities of fire-affected rock.

One of the most conspicuous aspects of SHA-1043 is the large number of ash features. These appear to be the remains of burned-out fires that were subsequently buried, or old ash dumps from cleaning out a hearth or oven. Anyone who has cleaned out a wood stove is familiar with this material; the ash is very light in color, ranging from white to

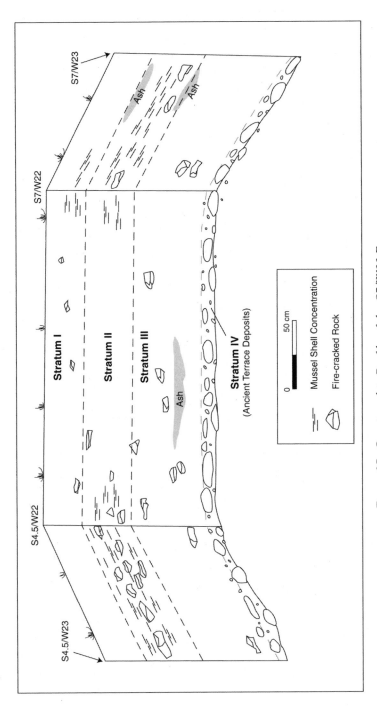

Figure 27. Stratigraphic Profile of the S7/W23 Exposure

light gray, and can sometimes yield important clues to the dietary practices of former inhabitants.

Cultural Features

Twenty domestic features were investigated at the site. These included the remains of three houses and one earthen lodge, a mussel-roasting oven, ten ash concentrations, four hearths, and an artifact cache. The following section describes a sample of these findings.

The Wintu House (Feature 3)

This feature was discovered by a backhoe trench when it clipped the top of some burned timbers. Four excavation units were then used to expose the house. The excavations progressed slowly, carefully exposing the burned timbers and leaving them pedestalled in place so we could determine the configuration of the structure. Almost all the timbers were fully exposed at eighty centimeters below the surface, and they were laying in a circular configuration (Figure 28), with the base of the timbers deeper than the ends, implying the conical shape of the original structure. It is interesting to note that the ends of the timbers were incomplete, having been burned; this was also the case for the covering of the house. These findings probably indicate that the house was fully engulfed in flame, which destroyed all but the thickest infrastructural components around its perimeter.

After recording the positions of the timbers, archaeologists removed them and continued excavating downward. At about one hundred centimeters below surface, they encountered the floor of the former structure, which measured about three meters (ten feet) in diameter. It was composed of hard-packed clay about three centimeters thick, with a very thin (two to three millimeters) surface of finer, slip-like clay, perhaps indicating that water had been used to smooth the floor during its construction. Although the floor was slightly concave, it did not appear to be a deep pit house.

A small rock-lined fireplace was found along the western edge of the house. Composed of flat rocks placed on end in a rectangular pattern, it was filled with white ash, similar to the ash concentrations found throughout the deposit. A small concentration of human bone was found on the floor in the center of the house, and we thought that there may have once been a burial pit at this location. Upon further investigation,

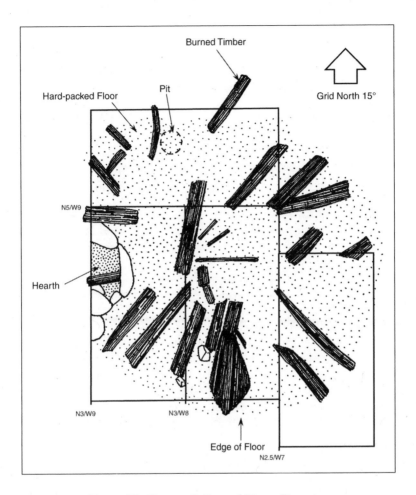

Figure 28. Feature 3, Burned House Remains

it was determined that a single body was laid directly on the floor of the house, without associated artifacts, and the structure was probably burned soon thereafter. Only 5 percent of the skeleton remained; it was collected and reburied on the "Conservancy parcel" (the preserved cemetery area). We do not know why this person hadn't been buried in the traditional way, but some of the Wintu working on the project suggested that the person may have died from a particularly severe disease that the living people had wanted to avoid.

Over time, archaeological deposits built up over the collapsed house, totally obscuring its existence. As a result, it's somewhat difficult to distinguish between artifacts that were originally in the house versus those associated with later occupations. The floor surface appeared to be quite clean of artifacts, as were the clay sediments used to manufacture the floor. Artifacts found ten centimeters above the floor, however, included nine projectile points, four flaked-stone tool fragments, one drill, one pestle, one milling stone, and seventy-eight pieces of animal bone.

A single radiocarbon sample was obtained from one of the timbers. It yielded a date of 184 BP (AD 1766), or sixty-six years before John Work's Hudson Bay Company trip through the area, the significance of which we'll discuss in Chapter V. The remains suggest a structure remarkably similar to the houses described by Cora Du Bois (Chapter III) and photographed by early visitors to the area (Figure 29).

Two other houses were discovered at the site but both were in poor condition. One was positioned at N5.5/W16—5.5 meters north and 16 meters west of the site datum (the point from which all site measurements are taken). Located at 100 to 120 centimeters below the surface, this house (labeled Feature 19) lacked preserved timbers, but it did have a circular floor (three meters in diameter) and a rock-lined hearth similar to that at the intact house (Feature 3). A third house (Feature 26) was found at S3.5/W12.5 at 120 to 140 centimeters deep. It was almost entirely destroyed by burial pits later created by the Wintu within the historic-period cemetery; only remnant pieces of the floor and hearth were left.

The Wintu Earthen Lodge (Feature 21)

The earthen lodge was discovered during the scraping phase of work, when the front loader exposed burned timbers. As a result of this finding, we excavated a trench just west of the burned timbers to expose the stratigraphic profile of the area (Figure 30). The upper zone (Stratum I) contained many large, burnt roof timbers and a significant amount of loose soil, which was probably part of an earthen roof. Stratum II was a fill zone composed of more timbers, a loose layer of river cobbles, and burnt soil and ash, probably representing the collapsed superstructure of the lodge. Stratum III was the hard-packed floor zone, and Stratum IV included subfloor midden deposits, which lay immediately above the ancient river terrace.

After clearing away peripheral deposits with the backhoe, four units

Figure 29. Traditional Wintu House Similar to Feature 3

were excavated over the top of the feature. The roof was encountered at about 60 centimeters below surface and included several large timbers (Stratum I, Figure 31). A small hearth also found on top of the timber zone was probably constructed and used after the lodge collapsed. After the timbers were exposed, photographed, and mapped, they were removed and the excavations continued into the fill zone between about 90 and 120 centimeters (Stratum II). Surprisingly, the cobbles observed in the initial stratigraphic profile turned out to be the remains of a large hearth associated with a poorly developed floor. They were found at a depth of 90 to 105 centimeters, well above the original floor zone (Figure 32). This finding indicates that the original lodge was reused at a later point in time, with a shallower living area lacking a well-defined floor. After removing the hearthstones, the original floor zone (Stratum III) was found at between 120 and 138 centimeters, with the actual

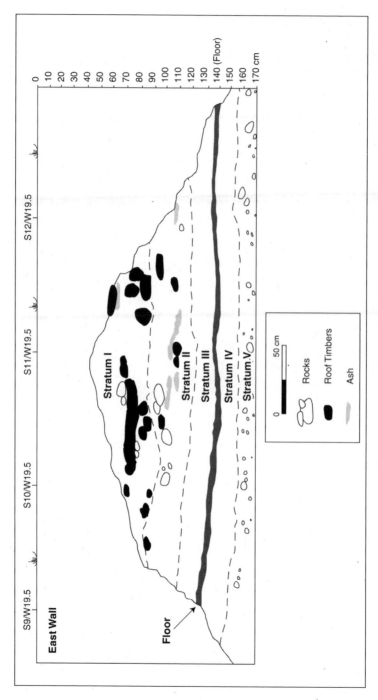

Figure 30. Stratigraphic Profile of Feature 21, Earthen Lodge

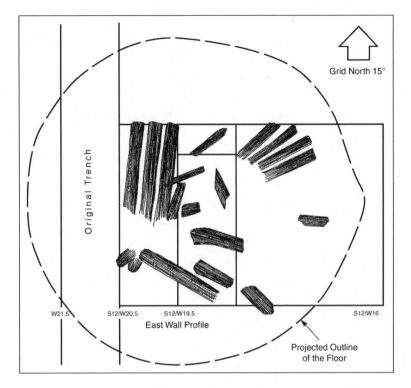

Figure 31. Plan View of Timber Zone (Stratum I; 70 cm)
at Feature 21, Earthen Lodge

hard-packed floor encountered at about 135 centimeters below surface.
A stone-lined fireplace was also discovered at the eastern edge of the
floor.

The original floor measures about 5.5 meters (18 feet) in diameter,
which falls within the 15- to 20-foot range for earthen lodges reported
by Du Bois (1935); it probably looked similar to an old photograph of a
lodge from neighboring Nomlaki territory (Figure 33). The artifact densities within these remains, which are relatively low throughout, are also
consistent with the function of Wintu lodges, which were used as men's
gathering places and shaman initiation venues but not for everyday
domestic activities. This relationship is best illustrated by comparing the
volume of artifacts found in the earthen lodge with that from midden
samples excavated less than five meters away; artifact densities equal 4.0
items per cubic meter in the lodge but as much as 14.4 per cubic meter
in the adjacent midden.

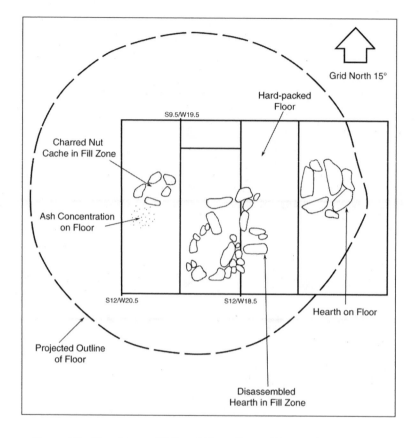

Grid North 15°

Hard-packed
Floor

S9.5/W19.5

Charred Nut
Cache in Fill Zone

Ash Concentration
on Floor

S12/W20.5   S12/W18.5

Hearth on Floor

Projected Outline
of Floor

Disassembled
Hearth in Fill Zone

Figure 32. Plan View of Fill and Floor Zones (Stratum III; 135 cm)
at Feature 21, Earthen Lodge

The two radiocarbon dates obtained from the feature clearly document the long-term use and reuse of the lodge. One sample came from the floor and produced a date of 935 BP (AD 1015), which may represent the earliest occupation at the site. The second sample came from a burnt timber at the top of the profile (Figure 34) and returned a date of 104 BP (AD 1846), reflecting use that could postdate the malaria epidemic of 1833, which will be discussed in detail in Chapter V. This latter date should be viewed with caution, however, as there are limits to the accuracy of radiocarbon dating; in fact, the AD 1846 date comes with an error factor of +/- thirty years, which could place the last use of the earthen lodge before the catastrophic epidemic. Given the lack of glass beads and other European trade goods within the lodge, a pre-contact occupation actually seems more likely.

Hearths and Ash Concentrations

Hearths differ from ash concentrations because the former are intact features (usually containing ash, charcoal, burned soil, and fired-affected rock) while ash concentrations appear to be the remains of cleaned-out hearths. Although every house at the site included a hearth, several other hearths were not associated with structural remains, which probably means that some cooking activities took place outside during the warm

Figure 33. An Earthen Lodge from Wintoon Territory

Figure 34. Close-up of Burned Timbers from
Feature 21, Earthen Lodge

seasons. One such hearth (Feature 15; N0.5/E5.5) included stratified layers of black charcoal and white ash overlaying a concentration of fire-affected rock. A flotation sample obtained from the feature contained a small amount of charred acorn nutshell and manzanita nuts and little else. Given that acorns were shelled before being used and that manzanita nuts were left over after the fruit was processed, it seems likely that these byproducts were not cooked in the hearths but disposed of there along with other unwanted waste.

A different situation was found at Feature 1, which appears to be the remains of a mussel-roasting hearth. It includes a concentration of fire-affected rock, white ash, and numerous burned fragments of freshwater shellfish. Analysis of the shell by archaeologist Tim Carpenter indicates that the pearl mussel (*Margaritifera falcata*) was the primary species harvested in the area, followed by lesser quantities of the Western ridge mussel (*Gonidea angulata*) and a small snail known as the scalloped juga (*Juga occata*). Men would dive for these mollusks in the river and consume them after roasting. Du Bois also notes that if the supply were plentiful, it was dried in basketry trays and stored for winter use.

Prehistorically, the freshwater mussel was widely distributed in the rivers and streams of northern California, favoring cold, rapidly moving water at depths of 0.5 to 1.5 meters (1.6 to 5.0 feet). They inhabited gravelly bottoms in protected areas, forming large beds, but twentieth-century land and water modifications have eradicated them from most of their previous habitats.

Of the twenty-five ash concentrations identified in the backhoe trenches, ten were formally sampled. Judging from the frequency with which they were found in the trenches, we predicted that there were somewhere between five hundred and one thousand total ash concentrations at the site; these numbers were roughly confirmed during the scraping phase of work. As mentioned above, these deposits are most likely the results of cleaned-out hearths and ovens. Their excavations revealed charred plant remains and little else; these contents will be discussed later in more detail, in the section titled "Plant Foods" (see page 70).

Radiocarbon Dates

Five radiocarbon dates were obtained from the site, three of which we discussed in previous sections (the Feature 3 house, dated at 184 BP, and the Feature 21 earthen lodge, dated at from 935 to 104 BP and covering various remodels). The two remaining dates come from olivella shell beads associated with the burials at the site that were thought to be the oldest based on their horizontal and vertical location. One (Burial 69) came in at 448 BP, while the other (Burial 2) dated to 330 BP; both fall within the range of the other three collected dates. These findings indicate that the site was occupied during relatively recent (i.e., Shasta Pattern) times, therefore postdating the arrival of the Wintu into northern California.

Projectile Points

If occupation of the site truly postdates 900 BP (AD 1050), then the projectile point styles we recovered from the site should match up with that period. As we discussed in Chapter II, six temporally diagnostic types exist in the local area: Borax Lake Wide-stemmed (8000–5000 BP), Squaw Creek Contracting-stemmed (5000–3000 BP), McKee Uniface (5000–3000 BP), Clikapudi Corner-notched (4000–1700 BP), Gunther Barbed (post 1700 BP), and Desert Side-notched (post 400 BP). It follows, therefore, that most of the points from this site should be Gunther Barbed or Desert Side-notched. As illustrated by Table 1, this is indeed the case for ninety-three out of the ninety-four points recovered from the village portions of the site (Figure 35). This finding is also consistent with the settlement-pattern data presented in Chapter II, which showed an abrupt settlement of riverine areas by Shasta Pattern/Wintu peoples at the time; this clearly happened at the site in question, as we found no trace of occupation there prior to 900 BP.

Beads

Certain types of shell beads can also be good temporal indicators. Of the two general types found in the village deposits, the olivella spire-lopped—so called because their tips (or spires) have been removed to allow the string to pass through the body cavity and out the new opening—are poor temporal indicators because they were popular in both prehistoric and historic times.

The other type of bead found at the site—clamshell disk beads, from the *Saxidomus* (Washington) clam—have much better temporal resolution. Cut from the shell wall of the clam and then perforated with a flaked-stone drill and ground on a stone into a disk shape, they tended to get larger over time; the smallest versions (A1) date to 450–250 BP,

Table 1. Projectile Point Frequencies from the Village at CA-SHA-1043

DEPTH (CM)	0-20	20-40	40-60	60-80	80-100	100-120	120-140	TOTAL
SHASTA PATTERN (POST 1500 BP)								
Desert Side-notched	1	1	-	2	1	2	-	7
Gunther Barbed	17	18	8	15	12	9	7	86
WHISKEYTOWN PATTERN (4000–1500 BP)								
Clikapudi	-	-	-	-	-	-	-	-
SQUAW CREEK PATTERN (5000–3000 BP)								
Squaw Creek/McKee	-	-	-	-	-	-	1	1
BORAX LAKE PATTERN (8000–5000 BP)								
Borax Lake Wide-stemmed	-	-	-	-	-	-	-	-
TOTAL	18	19	8	17	13	11	8	94

Gunther Barbed

Desert Side-notched

Figure 35. Projectile Points from the Village at CA-SHA-1043

the medium (A2) to 250–100 BP, and the large (A3) postdate 100 BP (or after AD 1850 and the arrival of Europeans to northern California). Our sample was limited to small- and medium-sized beads and lacked the larger, historic-period forms, patterning consistent with the other temporal indicators found within the village, which also lack historic markers like European trade goods.

PREHISTORIC TOOLS

Unfortunately for the archaeologist, many of the implements used by the Wintu were made out of perishable materials (for example, wooden bows, leather clothing, and basketry). Nevertheless, many of the preserved items made from harder materials like bone and stone were integral parts of more complex tools, allowing us to infer a wider range of technologies and activities that existed at the site. Four major categories of tools are recognized by archaeologists: flaked-stone tools, ground and battered stone implements, bone tools, and other miscellaneous items (Table 2).

Flaked-stone Tools

Obsidian was a preferred material for making flaked-stone tools. A type of volcanic glass, it forms a very sharp edge when it is broken. (Obsidian scalpels are now being produced on a commercial basis because their superior sharpness has led a growing number of surgeons to select them over the more commonly used stainless and carbon steel implements.) Most of the obsidian in the Upper Sacramento River drainage comes from two places: the Medicine Lake Highlands and the Tuscan Formation (Figure 36). Medicine Lake obsidian occurs as natural flows, and large chunks of high-quality material can be removed from the quarry with little effort. Tuscan, in contrast, occurs as smaller, low-quality cobbles and pebbles dispersed across the landscape. Because of these differences, Medicine Lake obsidian was traded widely across northern California during certain periods of prehistory, whereas the distribution of Tuscan obsidian was always limited to the local area.

The production and interregional exchange of Medicine Lake artifacts reached a pinnacle between 4000 and 1000 BP. During this heyday, the volcanic glass was processed using a biface reduction sequence (Figure 37). The sequence begins with a large core (a large chunk of obsidian), which is flaked through striking with a hard cobble on two sides (hence the term "biface"). An item is considered a Stage 1 biface

Table 2. Artifacts from the Village Deposits at CA-SHA-1043

FLAKED STONE				BONE TOOLS		GROUND/ BATTERED STONE		OTHER ITEMS	
TYPE	OBSIDIAN	METAVOLCANIC	OTHER	TYPE		TYPE		TYPE	
Projectile Points	93	-	3	Awls	17	Pestles	9	Shell Beads	17
Bifaces	100	4	1	Large Harpoons/Gorges	9	Mortars	5	Quartz Crystals	1
Drills	1	1	1	Small Harpoons/Gorges	7	Abraders	5	Pipes	1
Flake Tools	14	20	4	Gaming Pieces	1	Battered Cobbles	5		
Cores	8	91	2	Unique Items	3	Miscellaneous	2		
Core Tools	-	5	-	Fragments	27				

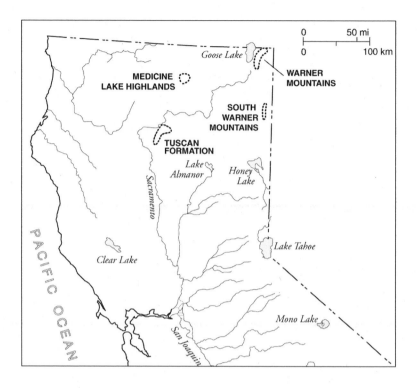

Figure 36. Key Obsidian Source Areas in Northern California

when only a few flakes have been removed; it is a Stage 2 biface when additional flakes have been removed and the object has taken on a more regular, oblong outline. A Stage 3 biface has been flaked through striking with a deer antler (called a "soft hammer"), has multiple flake removals, and is a nicely thinned preform. Stage 4 and 5 bifaces are further refined using pressure flaking, which is the process by which small flakes are removed through pushing them off with the tip of an antler; Stage 4 bifaces are near-finished blanks, and Stage 5 bifaces are finished tools. Because the flaking debris (also known as "debitage") reflects the type and stage of tool manufacturing that occurred at a site, archaeologists can precisely identify stoneworking activity from the debitage, even if the tools themselves have been removed from the site.

Evidence shows that stoneworkers usually made Stage 2 and Stage 3 bifaces at the Medicine Lake quarries and then carried them off for later use or exchange with nonlocal people, sometimes exporting these items more than one hundred miles from the quarry. Sometime around one

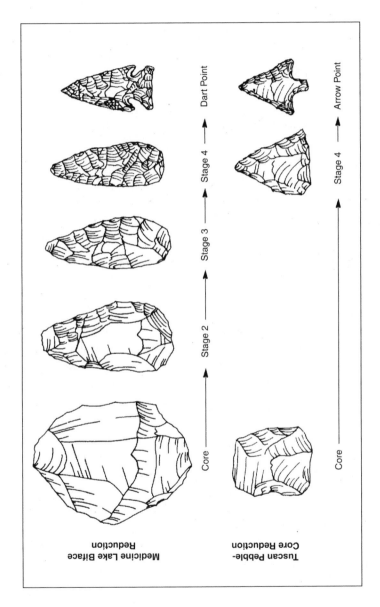

Figure 37. Alternative Flaked-stone Tool Production Strategies

thousand years ago, however, the Medicine Lake obsidian production and exchange system collapsed, and the spread of obsidian across the landscape retracted to the source. No one really knows why this happened, but some have speculated that the shift to bow-and-arrow technology lowered the demand for obsidian (arrow points require smaller pieces than darts), while others think that increased population and territoriality created less-amiable relationships between groups, resulting in the breakdown of traditional trade networks.

For whatever reason, Medicine Lake obsidian became less important over time and was replaced by local sources of stone, including Tuscan obsidian. This is clearly evidenced at SHA-1043, where a large proportion of obsidian imported to the site comes from the Tuscan source area. Although the small Tuscan pebbles could not be used to produce large obsidian tools, they were sufficient to make the small Gunther Barbed arrow points that were commonly found throughout the deposit.

Bone Tools

More than sixty bone tools and fragments were recovered from the site. They include awls (or pieces of broken awls), composite harpoon parts, a gaming piece, and several unidentifiable fragments. Although these artifacts are rather simple in appearance, they represent a wide range of activity, including the manufacture of garments and baskets (the awls), salmon fishing (the harpoon pieces), and lively gambling competitions (the gaming piece).

The awls were made from the lower leg bone of deer (the metapodial or cannon bone). An artisan split the bone down the middle by striking the top with a hammerstone and then ground the bottom into a sharp point (Figure 38). All of the tips were highly polished from use, and some had been hardened over a fire. According to Du Bois, they were typically used to sew clothing made from deerskin; the high-gloss polish on the implements is certainly consistent with that use.

Fishing gear also makes up a large portion of the bone tool assemblage. As outlined in Chapter III, the Wintu used a composite harpoon to catch salmon. The harpoons included wooden toggles that were tipped with sharp points made from bone. These little bone points are all that survive in the archaeological record (wooden shafts, sockets, and fiber rope all decompose), and appear to have been made in two sizes (Figure 38). The larger-sized points include blanks (uncompleted

Gaming Piece

Awl

Awl

Toggle Harpoon Tips

Figure 38. Bone Tools from CA-SHA-1043

pieces) and finished pieces, and range between fifty-five and thirty-three millimeters in length; the smaller-sized points range between twenty-eight and eighteen millimeters. Both groups look similar to those illustrated by Du Bois and may have served the same function. It is also possible that some were gorges used in hook-and-line fishing; Du Bois notes that thorns could be tied to the primary bone point to improve the quality of the hook but that this type of fishing was rare.

A final bone artifact of interest is a gaming piece fragment (Figure 38). Its complete end has been rounded through scraping and polishing, and it fits the description of the "ace" used in the *bohemtcus* ("big wood") hand game, one of the major gambling events in Wintu culture.

FOOD REMAINS

Food remains—including the charred fragments of plants and the butchered bones of animals—represent valuable sources of information on ancient societies. Not only can they inform us about the prehistoric Native American diet, they provide materials conducive to radiocarbon dating and can even help reconstruct environmental conditions deep into the past. While it is possible to determine the relative importance of different plant and animal foods in the Wintu diet, it is much more difficult to estimate the proportion of plant versus animal foods consumed at the site due to the differential rate of decomposition of these two types of remains (that is, plant remains decompose much faster than animal bones). As a result, plant and animal remains are analyzed separately.

Plant Foods

Plant remains found in archaeological deposits are usually small and quite fragile, making them difficult to collect using standard screen-sorting techniques. But because charcoal is extremely lightweight and will actually float in water, archaeologists can recover them using the flotation method.

Nine flotation samples from the site were processed, each composed of four liters of soil. The soil from each sample was carefully submerged and thoroughly mixed into a large container of water. The heavier contents (silt, sand, and gravel) sank to the bottom of the container, while the lighter elements (charred seeds, charcoal fragments) floated to the top, where they could be skimmed off the surface of the water and then scanned.

Identifiable seeds were initially sorted into two groups by size. Small seeds came from a variety of grasses and herbs that were gathered with seed beaters and baskets, similar in many ways to the harvest of modern wheat and other cereal crops. Large-seeded foods include acorns, pine nuts, and certain berries, like manzanita. Many of the large-seeded foods were greatly prized due to their high nutritional value and ability to be stored for extended periods of time.

The Wintu lived in an optimal environment for nut crops; gray pine nuts and multiple species of acorns were readily available in the local area. The dependence on these foods is illustrated by the findings from SHA-1043, where acorns, pine nuts, and manzanita make up over 90 percent of the collection (small seeds were only minimally present). Within the large-seeded assemblage, acorn nutshells made up 75.6 percent of the total, followed by lesser frequencies of manzanita nutlets and pine nutshell, with only trace amount of buckeye fragments (Figure 39). The significant presence of acorn, manzanita, and pine nuts is consistent with Du Bois's assessment of the Wintu diet, although the near-absence of buckeye is surprising given that it was thought to have been an important dietary staple (see Chapter III).

One of the most interesting finds at the site was a burned cache of seeds from the earthen lodge (Feature 21). Even though this structure was relatively clean of artifacts, particularly when compared to adjacent midden areas, it appeared that someone had stored seeds in a rock-lined pit just before the lodge was burned. The cache was remarkably well-preserved and included actual acorn meats (we usually only find the husks) from valley oak, blue oak, and interior live oak.

As for the collection of small-seeded plants, it was dominated by filaree, followed by lesser amounts of farewell-to-spring, brome grass, elderberry, goosefoot, and red maids. Most of these plants favor disturbed habitats, particularly those that have been burned. Controlled burning was a common practice throughout pre-contact California, as it increased the abundance of small-seeded plant foods, enhanced feed for deer and elk by removing woody material and creating new shrubby sprouts, and controlled insects and diseases that could damage wild foods. Indians in northern Nevada commonly burned immediately after harvesting, and sometimes they sowed goosefoot seeds across the burned areas. Although we have no direct evidence for this form of incipient cultivation in northern California, it probably occurred here occasionally as well.

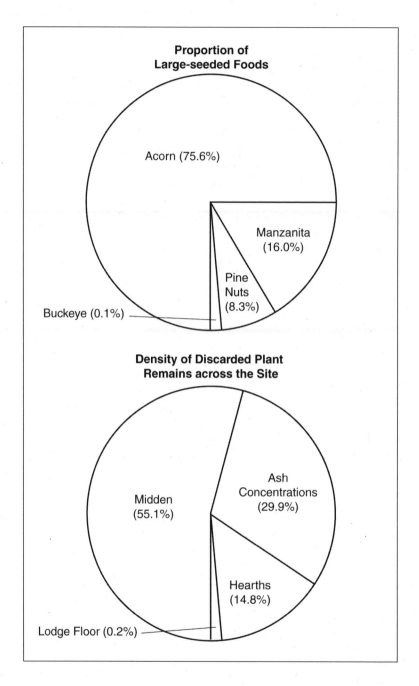

Figure 39. Charred Plant Remains from CA-SHA-1043

The distribution of plant remains across the site provides some interesting insights on the discarding behaviors of the people living there. Acorn hulls, pine nut shells, and manzanita nutlets were all considered garbage, so they were disposed of in fires, where they also produced a small amount of fuel. Flotation samples collected from the lodge floor, formal hearths, ash dumps, and the midden give us the answer (Figure 39). Practically no plant remains were found in the lodge floor, indicating that this area was kept quite clean. Seed densities are higher in formal hearths, but even these seem to have been regularly cleaned out, as evidenced by twice the density of charred seed waste in the ash dumps. Finally, maximum charred seed densities occur in the midden, probably a result of the innumerable informal outdoor firepits that were used over the centuries.

Filaree: European Plants Outpacing the Explorers?

Initial European entry into California was highly disruptive to the Native peoples, beginning with the introduction of devastating diseases (as we will see in the next chapter) and followed by the permanent settlement of the outsiders and their families. Recent analyses of plant remains from other Shasta County archaeological sites show that European weedy plants may also have been part of the invasion, spreading over much of the landscape even before the arrival of the settlers and their diseases.

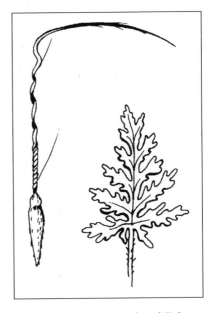

The major colonizing plant we see in the archaeological record is filaree (*Erodium cicutarium*), a weedy annual that spreads rapidly into open, disturbed habitats, including those that have been burned. Filaree has drill-like seeds (Figure 40), and most of the readers who have walked across California grasslands during the summer have had the occasion to pull some out of their socks. Its early presence was first

Figure 40. Filaree Seed and Foliage

discovered in pollen samples collected from the Santa Barbara Channel in sediments dating between 1750 and 1765. Historical biogeographers Scott Mensing and Roger Byrne made this discovery in the late 1990s and suggested that the plant was transported from Europe with livestock feed, then established itself near early Spanish settlements in Mexico, and later spread north into California even before the founding of the missions during the 1770s.

Archaeologist Eric Wohlgemuth has in recent years found evidence of filaree seeds in many northern California archaeological sites, some dating back to the 1600s, well before the findings from southern California. Is there the possibility of an earlier point of entry in northern California? The answer is yes. Several landfalls were made on the northern coast during the 1500s, the most famous being Sir Francis Drake in 1579. Drake's crew stayed in what is now Marin County for five weeks, and if he carried feed or bedding for livestock (pigs and chickens often accompanied the early stages of a voyage), or unprocessed grains for human use, then filaree seeds could have easily reached land. Whatever its origin point, filaree spread rapidly and became a significant food plant for the Wintu long before they encountered their first Europeans.

Animal Foods

Faunal remains, or the butchered bones of animals eaten by people at the site, also provide important information on the character of ancient diets, as well as insights into the condition of prehistoric environments. These materials were carefully collected from field screens and column samples and identified by archaeologist Tim Carpenter using a comparative skeletal collection. Many of the smaller bone fragments were unidentifiable (it is impossible to know what species of animal they came from), but those that could be identified were classified as to species, body part, and condition (for example, whether the piece had been burned or retained butchering marks).

The current collection is dominated by the remains of fish (49 percent) and mammals (48 percent), with only trace amounts of bird bone (Figures 41a and 41b). Mammals are represented by numerous species, including deer, elk, pronghorn antelope, jackrabbits, cottontails, and squirrels, but no bear (a surprising finding given the emphasis placed on these animals by the Wintu interviewed by Du Bois). The significant presence of elk and pronghorn is also quite interesting, as both species had been hunted to local extinction not too long after the abandonment of the site in the late 1800s. Although a large number of Wintu occupied this area and probably aggressively hunted elk and pronghorn, it wasn't until the arrival of Europeans and their guns that these animals were locally depleted.

A diverse mix of fish remains was also recovered from the site. Salmon and steelhead, the most popular types in the area, could be acquired in large numbers during major fish runs, and they represented about 50 percent of the fish samples from the site. The inhabitants of Kum Bay Xerel, however, also used many other species, perhaps supplementing their diets with local fishes during periods when salmon was less available. The Sacramento sucker, a bottom-feeder that occupies the river year-round, was one major contributor to the Wintu diet. Although they could have been harpooned individually, suckers are particularly abundant during their annual spawning within local tributaries in the early spring and could have been netted in greater numbers at that time (Figure 42).

Other important contributors to the diet include the hardhead and pikeminnow. Both of these fish feed in a variety of river habitats, and pikeminnow are known for eating juvenile salmon during their downstream migration to the sea. According to Peter Moyle, an expert on

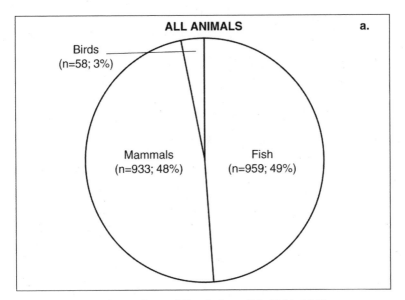

Figure 41. Animal Foods from CA-SHA-1043

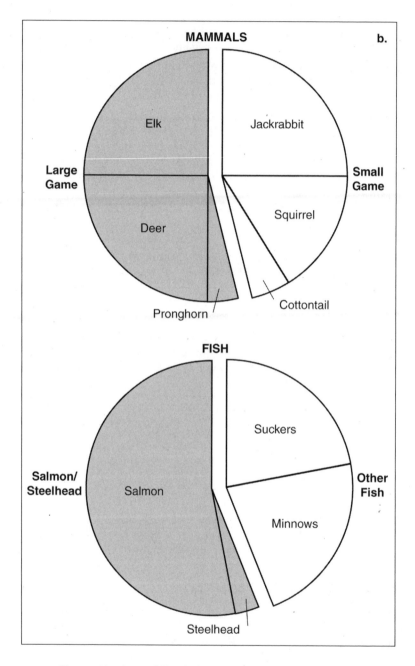

Figure 41. Animal Foods from CA-SHA-1043 *continued*

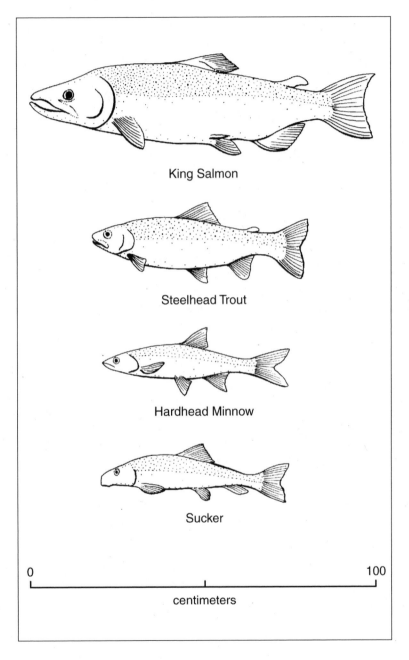

Figure 42. Fish Caught and Eaten at CA-SHA-1043

freshwater fishes of California, their predatory behavior can be problematic at the Redbluff Diversion Dam when most of the gates are closed to divert irrigation water into the Tehama-Colusa Canal and the mature pikeminnows consume the high concentrations of small salmon moving through the dam. Salmon and pikeminnow obviously coexisted rather well in earlier times given that they both represented an important food source for Wintu peoples living along the Sacramento River.

Discussion

Archaeological findings from the prehistoric village deposits at SHA-1043 reflect a lifestyle designed to make maximal use of the local environment. We encountered a wide range of tools used to hunt, fish, and process plants, as well as the charred and butchered remains of the foods consumed at the site. Exotic items traded in from distant places also supported the local economy, including obsidian tool stone from the Sierra-Cascade Range and clam bead money from the Pacific coast. This economic system supported a relatively large population for almost one thousand years, as documented by the multiple houses and large earthen lodge discovered at the site. As we will see in the next chapter, however, this way of life changed forever with the arrival of Europeans to northern California during the early 1800s.

Chapter V:
End of an Era:
First Contacts with Europeans

The Wintu lived in the Upper Sacramento Valley for at least one thousand years before encountering Europeans. At first the contact was sporadic, limited to a few visits by early Spanish explorers, such as Luis Antonio Argüello in 1821. Early diaries associated with these trips provide little detailed information about the local area but they all emphasize the presence of numerous Indian villages in the region.

Everything changed with the advent of the French-Canadian fur trade during the early 1800s. Enterprises like the Hudson Bay Company began trapping fur-bearing mammals in the far northern latitudes, moving south into Oregon and California in the 1820s and 1830s. One of the principal players in the Hudson Bay Company was John Work, who led several trapping expeditions out of Fort Vancouver (located across the Columbia River from present-day Portland), including a major trip to California. Unfortunately for many Indian groups living along low-lying river valleys, it appears that some of the Europeans who landed at Fort Vancouver were infected with malaria and, with the help of mosquitoes, spread the disease to thousands of Native people lacking sufficient immunities. The disease reached epidemic proportions in California during 1833, and for a long time, one of the only sources of information about this devastating year was John Work's diary. Now, we also have the physical remains of the people buried at SHA-1043.

We are quite lucky that John Work kept a detailed diary of the trip and that the log was not lost or destroyed along the way. The existence of the original manuscript remained largely unknown for many years, until Work's grandson told historian Alice Maloney that he remembered seeing it at his grandmother's house when he was a boy. Maloney later found and transcribed the diary and published it in multiple issues of the *California Historical Society Quarterly* in 1943 and 1944. It represents one of the most important documents of the early European–Native American contact period within California and Oregon.

JOHN WORK AND THE 1833 MALARIA EPIDEMIC

Fur trappers are usually thought of as mountain men working alone or in small groups. This was not the case for John Work. He was married to a woman named Josette Legrace (the daughter of a Nez Perce woman and a trapper) and, in addition to traveling with his wife and three daughters, he led on his 1832–1833 expedition to California one hundred men, women, and children. Most of the men were of European descent and had Indian wives from a wide range of geographic areas. The women processed the beaver and otter pelts and dried the meat of elk, deer, and bear that were hunted along the way and made up a large portion of their diet. Given that these expeditions were family enterprises, the children came along and helped out where they could. There were also several cases of Indian men serving as assistants to the trappers and hunters.

The brigade left Fort Vancouver on August 17, 1832, and headed east along the Columbia River to Fort Walla Walla (Figure 43). They then traveled due south across what is now eastern Oregon, reaching Goose Lake along the northeastern edge of California on October 22 and Fall River Valley, sixty-five miles east of Redding, on November 8. They camped on the Sacramento River at the mouth of Cow Creek on November 18 and decided to stay at this location for ten days to replenish their stocks of wild meat and build three dugout canoes for travel along the river.

During their stay at the Cow Creek camp, which was located across the river from present-day Anderson and only seven miles downstream from SHA-1043, they encountered numerous Indian people. All of the encounters were peaceful, and Work traded what he called "Trifles" (including glass beads) for local foods like dried salmon. The expedition also trapped thirty-five beaver and a single otter, and killed thirty deer, four elk, three pronghorn, two grizzly bears, and one black bear for food.

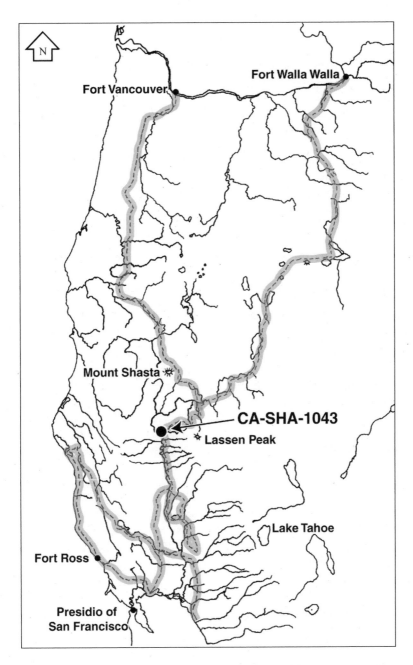

Figure 43. Route of John Work's Expedition to California, 1832–1833

Despite their peaceful interactions with local Indians, on one of their upstream trapping trips some of the men found a large village across the river (probably a Wintu settlement not far from SHA-1043) where the people had been attacked by Shasta Indians a few nights earlier. A few individuals had been killed and others carried off into slavery, and Work's men observed a cremation ceremony for the deceased. The entire village was abandoned a few days later.

The brigade continued south along the river where Work reported "a great many" Indians along the Sacramento and lower Feather Rivers. During a short day's journey he saw six villages ("the inhabitants of each must amount to some hundreds"); judging from these accounts, it's probable that this short stretch of river was populated by more than one thousand people. Although the Indian population seemed to be large and in good health, Work did note that along the Feather River "there appears to be some sickness resembling an ague [fever with chills] prevailing among them."

After waiting out multiple winter storms and flooding at the Sutter Buttes, the group spent several months traveling down to the Sacramento–San Joaquin Delta area, across the north end of San Francisco Bay, and up into the North Coast Ranges as far as the Eel River drainage. They came back to the Sacramento Valley crossing the Putah and Cache Creek drainages in late May of 1833 and encountered extreme heat and swarms of mosquitoes. From June 1 to early August, in fact, Work mentions "Musquitoes" on a regular basis, writing of "swarms… which are like to devour us" (June 6) and "swarms…so numerous last night that the people slept very little" (June 11).

The first mention of sickness within the Work brigade comes on July 31, when a few members of the party came down with a fever. The next day, moving north into the Feather River country, Work notes that, "A great many of the Indians are sick some of them with the fever." On August 6 he wrote:

Some sickness prevails among the Indians on feather river, The villages which were so populous and swarming with inhabitants when we passed that way in Jany or Febry last seem now almost deserted & have a desolate appearance. The few…who remain…are lying apparently scarcely able to move, It is not starvation as they have considerable quantities of their winter

stock of acorns remaining. We are unable to learn the malady
or its cause.

Farther north things appear to be worse among the Indian people
probably living just north of Chico. The suddenness and thoroughness
of the disease is staggering, as it appears that there were not enough
people left to bury the dead.

> The natives along here seem even more wretched than those
> on feather river, the villages seem almost wholly depopulated...
> [they] are found in ones or twos in little thickets of bushes, and
> the men found two one of whom was dead & the other nearly
> so. The bodies of others were partly devoured by the wolves...
> Here there is the materials for a fishing wear [weir] collected &
> prepared but [the people were] unable to construct it [August
> 14].

The condition of Work's group also declined, with fifty-one stricken
by August 18. They suffered from pains in their bones, violent head-
aches, and shaking fits at regular intervals. Upon reaching Battle Creek
on August 20 a young boy had died and the number of sick increased
to sixty-one. Moving up to Cow Creek, Work himself becomes sick and
worried if everyone would ultimately suffer the same fate as the Indians.
By August 25, seventy-two people were ill and an elderly Caiause Indian
named Berdach had died.

Things had begun to improve upon reaching the mountains near
Hat Creek, where the cooler weather helped with the fevers. The local
Indian populations seemed to be relatively healthy (probably due to living upland, away from the swarming mosquitoes) but they were not very
friendly. Although they traded berries for beads, the local Indians (probably the Achumawi) stole the company's horses on multiple occasions
during the first days of September. The sickened party left California on
September 12 and struggled back to Fort Vancouver, finally arriving on
October 29, 1833.

Additional evidence for this devastating epidemic comes from visits
to the area during the late 1830s and early 1840s. Accounts of these
trips were summarized by S. F. Cook in 1956 and reiterate the speed
and widespread nature of this sickness, noting the abandonment of multiple villages and, in some cases, the inability of the survivors to bury
all the dead. A year after Work's trip, the explorer Charles Wilkes saw

human bone scattered across the landscape, "there not being enough of the Tribe spared—as we were told—to bury the dead." Cook's analysis of these accounts led him to conclude that at least 75 percent of the valley population was lost during this disaster. This probably included those living at SHA-1043.

Archaeology of the Primary Cemetery Area:
Evidence for the Malaria Epidemic?

The sequence of discovery during our excavations at SHA-1043 is eerily parallel to the site's history of occupation. The initial backhoe trenching, hand excavations, and scraping found only prehistoric materials—including the prehistoric cemetery off the edge of the midden, similar to the one described by Du Bois. The vast majority of findings reflect successful village life for several hundred years and reveal no evidence of historical materials like glass beads, nor any hint of a devastating epidemic. This all changed, however, when we began excavating in a small portion of the deposit at about S5/W12. Here, within an area measuring only seven by seven meters, we found the remains of well over one hundred people—some probably representing the catastrophic loss of life associated with the malaria epidemic (Figure 44).

Excavation of human remains is a slow, delicate task. Once a burial is encountered, the archaeologist carefully digs with a trowel around its perimeter to define the horizontal and vertical extent of the skeleton; this effort will leave a block of soil encasing the remains. It is then necessary to remove the soil from around the bones so that its posture can be determined. Careful removal of soil is also required to obtain an accurate look at any associated artifacts, like a shell bead necklace, or arrow points embedded in the body.

After the skeletons were exposed and photographed (the latter with permission from the Most Likely Descendant), the bones from each individual were removed and kept together for analysis. During the current project, the age and sex of each individual was determined at the field lab by archaeologist Jim Nelson, one of the top field osteologists in the state. He also made several observations regarding the health of the individuals at the times of their deaths and whether they had experienced traumatic injuries during their lives. All of the associated artifacts were described and photographed on site. After these tasks were completed, all of the skeletal remains were returned to the landowner, Dave Abbott, and the Most Likely Descendant, Kelli Hayward, for

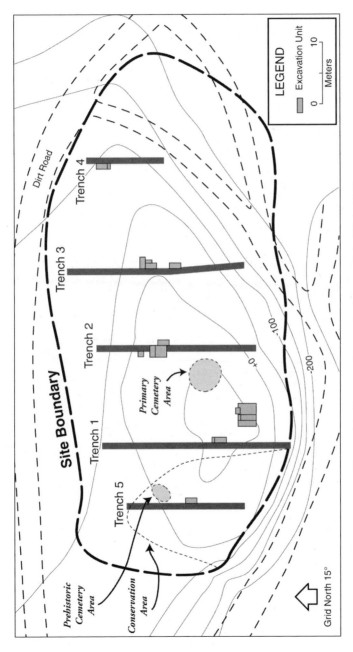

Figure 44. Primary Cemetery Area at CA-SHA-1043

reburial within the conservation area on the western margin of the site. A detailed accounting of all of these materials is available to qualified persons at the Northeastern Information Center at California State University, Chico.

Dating the Primary Cemetery Area

If the primary cemetery area reflects the 1833 malaria epidemic, what chronological information should we find? The most obvious items would be European trade items like the "Trifles" referred to by John Work. As demonstrated by Table 3, we indeed found European trade items, including more than fifty-three hundred glass beads. Of the twenty-nine burials containing glass beads, nine contained other items of European origin. These included an axe head, spoons, knives, buttons, metal cups, and a Hudson Bay Company copper kettle (Figure 45). The kettle is particularly noteworthy because it could represent a direct connection with John Work. Covered copper kettles were a major trade item used by the Hudson Bay Company due to their great popularity with Native peoples. They decreased cooking time by trapping the heat and decreasing evaporation, and they were also useful for storage. The kettle discovered during this excavation looks similar in size and manufacture to a three-quart Hudson Bay kettle commonly traded during the early 1800s.

Table 3. A Comparison of Artifacts from the Village
and the Cemetery at CA-SHA-1043

	VILLAGE	CEMETERY	TOTAL
FLAKED-STONE TOOLS	348	166	514
BONE TOOLS	64	39	103
GROUND/BATTERED STONE	26	36	62
BEADS			
Shell	17	2,775	2,792
Glass	-	5,320	5,320
Nut/Shell	-	32	32
PROJECTILE POINTS			
Gunther Barbed	86	79	165
Desert Side-notched	7	24	31
TOTAL	548	8,471	9,019

0   inches   5

Figure 45. Hudson Bay Company Covered Copper Kettle

Glass Beads

Glass beads are more difficult to link directly with the Hudson Bay Company because they were used by multiple groups in California at the time of historic contact. The Spanish brought them to central and southern California during the height of the Mission period (roughly 1770 to 1820). They were also traded by members of the Russian-American Company at Fort Ross in Sonoma County between 1812 and 1841, and by the Hudson Bay Company on expeditions from Fort Vancouver from 1829 to 1860. Although they represent distinct ethnic groups from vastly different parts of Europe, most of the trade beads used by explorers and settlers came from the same place—Venice, Italy. Venetian glass factories held a global monopoly on glass bead production for hundreds of years, beginning in the fourteenth century, and supplied all of the merchant exporters who ultimately distributed them to Native peoples all over the world.

We know very little about how the shapes and colors of these beads changed over time because the Venice monopolies kept their manufacturing technologies and production schedules under strict secrecy to prevent others from entering the business. Moreover, some popular types were manufactured for long periods of time, and inventories of others were kept in storage for many years before entering the global market. Thus it is not possible to classify different bead types according to their date of manufacture and then use these beads to precisely date the archaeological deposits in which they were found. The beads do, however, provide an excellent measure of the first contacts with Europeans in the region.

Three basic types of glass beads were found at the site: drawn, wound, and mold-pressed. Drawn beads are manufactured by drawing or stretching molten glass into long canes that are then cut and shaped. Wound beads are produced by wrapping molten glass around a wire. Mold-pressed beads are made by pressing the heated glass into a two-piece mold. The beads were either made from a single color of glass (monochrome) or layered with glass of different colors (polychrome). Some take a simple rounded form while others have elaborate faceting (Figure 46).

In 1976, archaeologist Lester A. Ross studied the glass beads found in deposits at Fort Vancouver, providing us with an inventory of the bead types John Work may have used on his trip to California. Most of the drawn and wound beads found at Kum Bay Xerel are quite similar to those found at Fort Vancouver and, like the Hudson Bay kettle, probably reflect contact with Work's expedition. The mold-pressed beads could mark a separate event, however, as they were specialized items manufactured in Czechoslovakia, and may have entered the market slightly later than the other beads (i.e., sometime in the mid-1830s).

While the presence of these beads indicates that much of the primary cemetery dates to the time of John Work (or soon thereafter), and

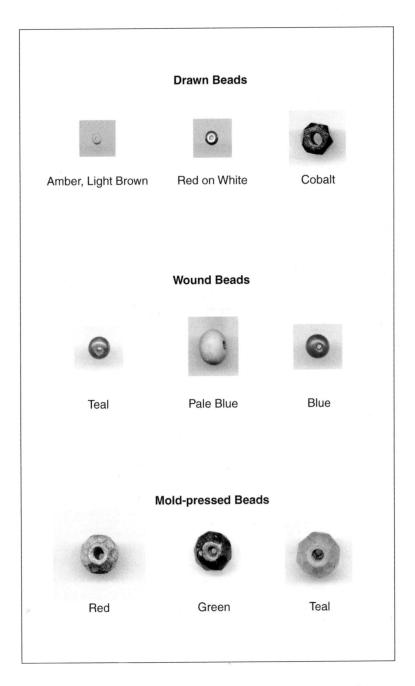

Figure 46. Glass Trade Beads from CA-SHA-1043 (full scale)

postdates the occupation of the main village area, where no glass beads were found, the question remains as to whether all of the interments correspond to the malaria epidemic. This question can be answered by comparing the frequency of glass beads to the frequency of accompanying grave goods dated to earlier periods. Glass beads obviously date to the historic period, whereas clam disk beads start at about 500 BP, extending into the historic period, and olivella beads can be even older.

When we sort the individual burials according to their associations with the three bead types (a process called "seriation"), we find that glass beads were not found in every grave (Figure 47). Instead, three general groups emerge: one with mostly glass beads, another with mostly clam disk beads, and the third dominated by olivella beads. The glass bead group of graves had an average depth of 123 centimeters, while the clam disk and olivella bead graves were slightly deeper, at an average of 138 and 152 centimeters, respectively. We also have a radiocarbon date of 448 BP from the olivella group (Burial 69), which indicates that most of these deeper graves predate the arrival of John Work and probably correspond to the main prehistoric occupation of the site. The age of the clam disk bead group is difficult to know, but it probably spans the prehistoric-historic transition. This supposition is supported by a radiocarbon date of 330 BP from a clam disk bead burial (Burial 2) discovered in another part of the site.

Treatment of the Dead

According to John Work's diary, and the writings of other people who traveled through the area soon thereafter, the devastating speed of the malaria epidemic made it difficult for tribal members to bury all of their deceased in a traditional manner. Was this also the case at SHA-1043?

Du Bois provides a detailed summary of traditional Wintu burial customs. Graveyards were situated about one hundred meters from the houses, and the locations of individual graves was determined by older members of the group who could remember where previous burials were made. If, however, they found bones from an earlier grave while digging a new one, the remains were wrapped in deer hide and reburied next to the new body. The bodies were put in flexed, crouching positions, wrapped in a deerskin or bear hide, and tightly bound with rope or sinew. Various personal items, including beads, were sometimes placed with the body. The grave pit was often lined with pine bark, and rocks were laid on top of the body prior to its being covered with dirt.

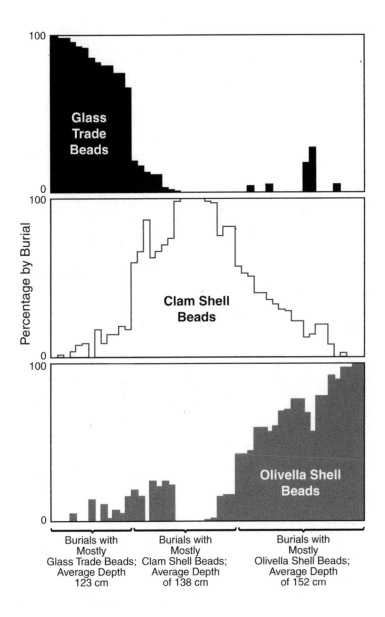

Figure 47. Relative Percentage of
Glass, Clam, and Olivella Shell Beads by Burial

The initial, prehistoric cemetery found on the edge of the midden deposit at SHA-1043 reflects this traditional approach to burial. We found tightly flexed individuals in sitting positions placed in bark-lined pits and covered with rock. Within the primary cemetery area, there was a mixture of traditional burials and mass graves lacking the details of formal grave preparation.

The traditional burials tended to be deeper than the more recent, nontraditional interments, and did not appear to have contained glass beads, which means they probably predated the arrival of John Work and the malaria epidemic. Judging from the high number of individuals and rocks found within such a small area, the location may have functioned as a mausoleum. Each new grave was probably dug around an existing rock cairn, with the body placed in the bark-lined pit and covered with more rock and soil. Although it is surprising that this activity apparently occurred in the middle of the village, there is no doubt, given the historical accounts of Du Bois, that it was used as a formal cemetery for a long time, and probably served as the resting place for multiple generations of related people. Over the years it was continually built up with rock cairns, eventually taking on semiformal architectural characteristics (Figure 48).

Probably a result of the mass deaths associated with the malaria epidemic, everything changed soon after the initial contact with Europeans. Nontraditional burials (lacking rock cairns and bark), frequently containing glass beads and other European items, have been found at variable depths although they tend to be shallower than the older ones. The urgency of these interments is further reflected by the burial of several individuals within a single grave pit, which often disturbed the bones of people who were buried in prehistoric times. In fact, a significant percentage of all the human remains found at the site had been disturbed by Wintu graves dug after the time of John Work.

A particularly moving interment was discovered on the north side of the cemetery: three people were found side by side, each in a loose sitting position, with their arms wrapped around one another. They appeared to be facing Mount Shasta, a orientation common for burials at the site. The remains were identified as a female between thirty-seven and forty-one years of age, a male nineteen to twenty-four years old, and a subadult of unknown sex. Given the age of these individuals and their simultaneous deaths, it seems likely that that they succumbed to the

Multiple Cairns Exposed in the Primary Cemetery Area

Close-up of Two Rock Cairns

Figure 48. Structural Characteristics of the Cemetery Area

epidemic and that there was neither the time nor energy to bury them individually, in the traditional manner.

Age of the Dead

If many of the historic-period Wintu burials found at the site represented a population impacted by an epidemic, then we should see differences in the age distributions between the prehistoric and historic populations at the site.

When estimating the age profile of a hunter-gatherer population like the Wintu, it is important to remember that high rates of infant mortality were common around the world until the development of modern antibiotics and vaccines helped eliminate many lethal childhood diseases. Analysis of the prehistoric interments from SHA-1043 shows that infants (up to five years of age) made up 17 percent of the cemetery population, after which the mortality rate dropped significantly: 4 to 7 percent for the individuals ages five to twenty (Figure 49). The number of deceased between the ages of twenty and thirty picked up again (16 to 22 percent), this due to increased risks associated with childbearing (women) and interpersonal violence (mostly young men). The percentage of people in the thirty to thirty-five age range dropped again, but increased between forty and forty-five, which in many cases was due to old age. Those who lived past forty-five—and some even to fifty-five—must have been greatly respected for their superior experience and knowledge.

Infant mortality was significantly higher (25 percent) after the arrival of John Work, and it stayed quite high within the five-to-ten group (20 percent), probably due to the malaria epidemic (Figure 49). Numbers were low within the ten-to-fifteen and fifteen-to-twenty groups, and mortality jumped again within the twenty-to-twenty-five interval, although not to the same degree as within the prehistoric population. Mortality rates were similar before and after contact for those aged twenty-five to forty, but numbers spiked again between forty and forty-five, which accounts for all the remaining members of the population.

This information can be more usefully graphed according to the probability of death for each age group. For this analysis, we first compute the percentage of the population still living at each age interval, beginning at 100 percent between birth and five years of age, and decreasing with each death across the age groups. We then calculate the

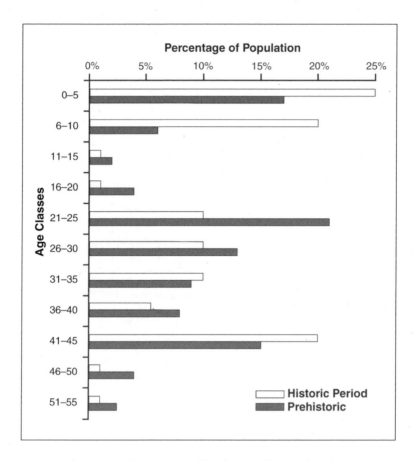

Figure 49. Percentage of Each Age Class within the
Primary Cemetery at CA-SHA-1043

probability of death by dividing the number of fatalities within each age class by the remaining number of people still alive within that same age class.

The probability of death data (Figure 50) for the historic Wintu population showed that infants (up to five years old) and juveniles (five to ten years old) took the brunt of the disease. By age ten, however, data for the historic population largely parallels that of the prehistoric population, except for the lack of people living past age forty-five, which probably signals greater vulnerability to malaria among the older people in the group. These findings indicate that the epidemic most greatly affected the young and the old, and that teenagers were able to withstand

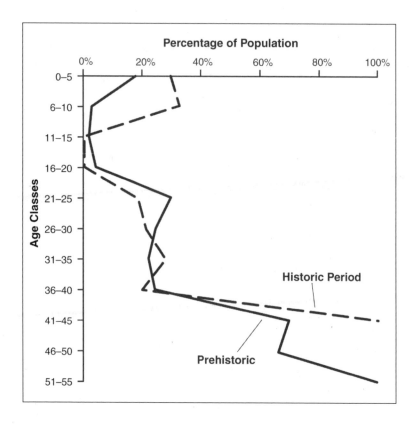

Figure 50. Probability of Death by Age Class at CA-SHA-1043

the effects of the disease better than any other age group. As we shall see shortly, the survivors showed a great deal of perseverance, as they were able to move into the future with much of their culture intact.

Males, Females, and Interpersonal Violence

One of the most surprising findings of the mortality analysis was the large number of people dying between the ages of twenty and twenty-five. These were the most frequent deaths in the prehistoric population at SHA-1043, and they occurred in much higher proportion than in other populations studied elsewhere in California. We know that mortality goes up among women in this age class due to the physical difficulties associated with pregnancy and childbirth, particularly in the absence of modern medicine (at the time it was one of the most dangerous things a woman could do); and for men between the ages of twenty and twenty-

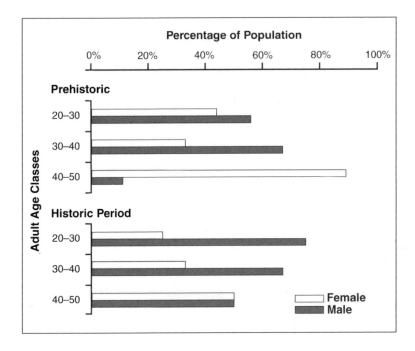

Figure 51. Percentage of Adult Males and Females
by Age Class at CA-SHA-1043

five, the mortality rate was influenced to varying degrees by warfare. We will now turn our attention to the adult population at Kum Bay Xerel in an attempt to further unravel the high mortality rate among the prime-age people living at the site.

Figure 51 provides sex ratios by age group for people buried at the site. Although female mortality during the reproductive years was significant, many more males than females were dying between the ages of twenty and forty within both the prehistoric and historic populations. After the age of forty, female deaths equalled or surpassed male deaths in both periods, probably because there were fewer men in the overall population.

But why were so many men dying at such a young age? The answer lies in the signs of trauma found on their skeletons. When all of the burials from the site are combined into a single group, we find that 63 percent of the men aged twenty to thirty showed evidence of trauma (both lethal and non-lethal)—more than three times the frequency of

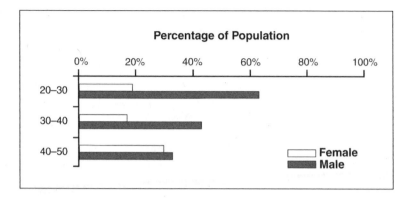

Figure 52. Percentage of Population (Historic Period and Prehistoric) with Traumatic Injuries According to Sex

trauma for women of the same ages (Figure 52). At the thirty-to-forty interval, trauma frequency began to drop (43 percent), ultimately reaching a low of 33 percent between forty and fifty years of age. These declining frequencies probably indicate that men who were able to avoid violent deaths during their twenties had a better chance of surviving longer and dying in their later years from more natural, nonviolent causes.

Depression fractures to the head were the most common form of trauma suffered by men, accounting for the majority of the injuries observed. These wounds left circular indentations in the skull and were the result of being clubbed. In a few cases the skull fracture killed the individual, but in many cases the bone had healed, indicating that some of these violent interactions were non-lethal in nature. Despite the relatively high frequency of survival after club trauma, the blows would have probably rendered the victims unconscious and in need of significant recuperation time. Females, although less prone to violence overall, were also subjected to clubbing, with cranial depression fractures accounting for over 80 percent of their injuries as well. Although it is difficult to determine the exact causes of this specific form of violence, it seems likely that the Wintu were having ongoing battles with their neighbors, probably due to maintaining or expanding their territorial boundaries.

Perhaps the most extreme examples of violence observed at the site—and one that provides additional evidence of warfare—were the executions or ambushes of three individuals. One of them, Burial 59, was a young man between nineteen and twenty-two years old who appeared to be relatively wealthy given the elaborate range of items he was buried with. He wore five abalone pendants and multiple necklaces adorned with over fifty shell and pine nut beads; he also had two bone awls that may have been used to make nets. His body was riddled with thirty projectile points (almost all Gunther Barbed), at least two of which had embedded in his vertebrae.

Other significant killings were found in the Burial 86 complex, where it appears that three people were buried together and mixed with the remains of two others interred at an earlier date. One of the people (86e) was a well-to-do man aged twenty-one to twenty-four with at least two necklaces totaling 380 shell beads, one strung with large clam disk beads and the other with smaller versions of the same type; five abalone pendants were also found with him. He was shot with fifteen projectile points, most lodged around his abdomen. The points included a strange mixture of Gunther Barbed, Desert Side-notched, and what appear to be nonlocal corner-notched types (similar to those found across the river in Yana territory). He also had a large obsidian knife near his groin, but it's unclear if it was a grave offering or if it had been embedded in his body.

In the same complex, Burial 86d was a male twenty-three to twenty-five years old buried with only a few beads. He was also riddled with almost twenty arrow points, most of them Desert Side-notched.

Given that some of these individuals were killed with multiple arrows (including those made by neighboring groups) but not stripped of their wealth, they most likely died while away from the village. After the bodies were recovered from the battlefield and brought back home, the belongings of the deceased, which had been safely stored at the village, were placed in their graves. The fact that these young men represented some of the wealthiest individuals in the cemetery, particularly Burials 59 and 86e, testifies to their importance among their fellow villagers. If so, we may be observing the burial of heroes in a society that highly esteemed its warriors.

Although it has been traditionally thought that most California Indians lived in peaceful coexistence, the burial findings at SHA-1043 indicate that intergroup conflict was quite common among the Wintu, both in prehistoric and historic times. In many ways, this should not be too surprising given the linguistic data presented in Chapter II, which shows that the Wintu were actively expanding their territory for a very long time. Even deep within their homeland along the Sacramento

River they must have needed to defend their rich resource base, where salmon, acorn, pine nuts, and many other foods co-occurred in abundances not seen in surrounding areas. The high value of this land, which continues to be the case today, was probably controlled at great cost, requiring young men to spend considerable time and energy defending it, often with their lives.

Rich People, Poor People

Many hunter-gatherer people throughout the world are largely egalitarian; that is, there is little difference among community members in the amount of wealth and power they possess. The Wintu were far from egalitarian, as they exhibited significant differences in wealth across the population. Historical accounts by Du Bois discussed in Chapter III indicate that they were socially stratified, with both rich and poor people living in the same community.

Can differential wealth within the community be seen in the cemetery at Kum Bay Xerel? The answer is a resounding yes. When we look at the percentage of people buried with beads and ornaments, and in differing amounts, we find that a minority of people possessed the vast majority of wealth (Figure 53). Among the prehistoric graves, 60 percent contained ten or fewer items of wealth, whereas 10 percent contained between one hundred and six hundred items of value. In fact, only 25 percent of the population had over 90 percent of the wealth. This discrepancy only increased after historic contact (when glass beads were added into the system), when more than 90 percent of the wealth was concentrated with only 10 percent of the people.

So who were the wealthiest members of the community? The two richest people in the prehistoric cemetery included the previously discussed male in his early twenties found with fifteen arrow points in his abdomen (Burial 86e) and, surprisingly, an infant less than one year old and of indeterminate sex (Burial 84). The infant was wrapped in what appears to have been a shawl that had over 340 olivella shell beads sewn into it; the baby also had an abalone pendant and a necklace made from seven Glycimeris shell beads, probably originally placed around its neck. When considering the expense associated with transporting all of those beads from their origin on the coast into Upper Sacramento River country, and the great care and skill it took to create the shawl, the child must have been a member of a very wealthy family.

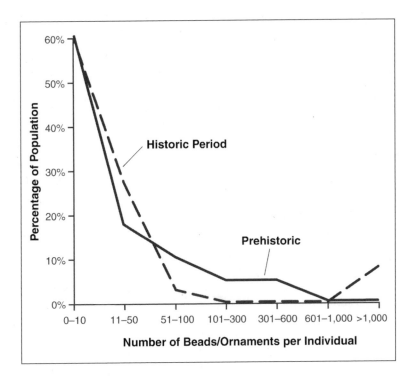

Figure 53. Percentage of Population (Historic Period and Prehistoric)
Buried with Beads and Ornaments

The two wealthiest people in the post-contact cemetery included an adult male (Burial 58a) and an adolescent eight or nine years old and of indeterminate sex (Burial 42). The male had 2,264 simple drawn-glass beads (mostly white and amber brown) that appear to have been strung into a necklace. Eight projectile points (both Gunther Barbed and Desert Side-notched) were placed in his grave, along with a grooved stone used to straighten arrow shafts, perhaps indicating that he had been an accomplished hunter. He also had a metal knife and some metal can fragments that were probably used as a cup.

The adolescent must also have come from an important family, as he or she was buried with the most riches and accumulation of material at the site. Every type and color of glass bead found at the site was found with this person, including the molded beads, which could indicate that this burial postdates by a few years the height of the malaria epidemic.

Most of the beads appear to have been originally buried in a textile pouch, which also had beads woven onto its exterior. Other historic-period artifacts in the grave included a metal clasp inlayed with glass beads, two wooden buttons, three metal buttons (brass and copper), metal garment fasteners, nails wound with string, an axe head, a metal spoon with a bone handle, and some metal cans that were also probably used as cups.

Other Historic-period Artifacts

Most of the archaeological information obtained from SHA-1043 indicates that it was abandoned soon after the 1832–1833 malaria epidemic. Artifacts postdating this era are essentially absent, which is consistent with Wintu elder Norel-putis not knowing about the site when Jeremiah Curtin interviewed him in the 1880s about local village locations. An interesting exception to this pattern was the discovery of an old pistol and powder case on the southeastern edge of the midden deposit, far away from the cemetery area. The gun appears to be a .54 caliber United States Military pistol issued in 1842 (Figure 54). The powder case is made from copper and has a hunting scene embossed on its face; its age is unknown (Figure 55). We don't know who owned these objects and whether he was Wintu or someone from outside the area. These items do, however, indicate that the site may have been occupied by at least a small number of people after the larger village was no longer used.

OTHER SITES IN THE AREA

Over the years, several Shasta Pattern sites have been excavated along the Upper Sacramento Valley due to impacts from modern developments. Data generated from eleven of these sites show the presence of rich prehistoric village deposits similar to those found at Kum Bay Xerel. Six also have evidence of European artifacts, but very few appear to represent the mass burial events evidenced here. Instead, most appear to represent Wintu settlements postdating the 1830s epidemic, probably reflecting a significant rebound in population, perhaps fueled by the large numbers teenagers who survived the malaria outbreak and others who had moved into the riverine settlements from upland areas largely unaffected by the mosquito-borne disease.

Trudy Vaughan, a local archaeologist, has studied this information in recent years and found only one site (SHA-237) that may be about the same age as Kum Bay Xerel, judging from the mixture of European and Native artifacts found at the site. Most of the other area sites (e.g.,

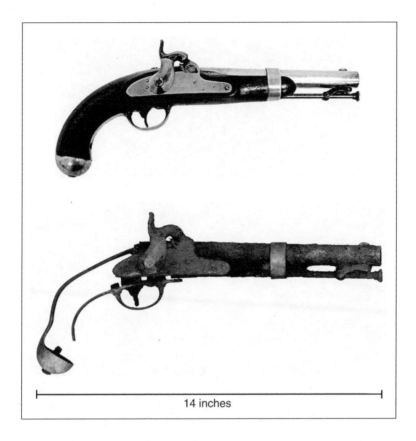

Figure 54. United States 1842 Military Pistol Compared to the
Gun Discovered at CA-SHA-1043

SHA-218, SHA-2830) were dominated by artifacts dating to the late 1850s and early 1860s (including coins and tools associated with the gold rush), and one (SHA-46) shows a continuance of Wintu traditions spanning the interval between 1850 and 1900.

DISCUSSION

Our excavations at SHA-1043 illustrate the rich information available in the archaeological record, and how it can increase the accuracy of early historical and ethnographic accounts. Until now, evidence for the 1832–1833 malaria epidemic was based on a few diaries written by people passing through the area, which led subsequent scholars to estimate that 75 percent of the local Native American population may

Figure 55. Copper Black Powder Flask
Discovered at CA-SHA-1043

have perished as a result. Although the rate of death increased significantly at this time, findings from the primary cemetery area indicate that the 75 percent estimate may be too high. Death rates were quite high among the youngest and oldest members of the Wintu population, but the survival rate of teenagers and individuals in their early twenties appears to have been much higher than originally thought.

The degree of violence exhibited in the cemetery population also exceeded our expectations, which were based on early ethnographic accounts of the Wintu. Most people are under the impression that California Indians were largely a peace-loving people, and that smalltime warfare occurred on only an occasional basis. This was not the case at SHA-1043. In fact, the cemetery contained the bodies of six times as many men between the ages of twenty and thirty as between ages thirty and forty, and the majority of the former group showed evidence of violent trauma on their bones. Although our findings represent a small fraction of the larger Wintu archaeological record, this high percentage of young, prime-aged men in the cemetery could reflect severe and persistent warfare over much of the Upper Sacramento Valley region, and should make students of California prehistory reevaluate their preconceived notions about war and peace in ancient cultures.

Chapter VI:
Summary and Conclusions

The Upper Sacramento River region experienced a rich, dynamic history spanning at least eight thousand years before European contact. Between about 8000 and 5000 BP the Borax Lake Pattern was prevalent in much of northern California. The people of that ancient culture followed a highly mobile settlement strategy, in which small family bands moved across multiple environmental zones over a yearly cycle but tended to spend most of their time in upland areas surrounding the Sacramento Valley. Their primary tools included large spear points—reflecting an emphasis on large-game hunting—and rather simple milling implements used to process a wide variety of plant foods.

At about 5000 BP, cultural diversity began to increase in northern California, probably due to the arrival of peoples from other parts of North America. A new culture, labeled by archaeologists as the Squaw Creek Pattern, employed atlatl and dart technology for the first time in the area, increasing overall hunting efficiency. Although they lived in larger groups and were slightly less mobile than their predecessors, the Squaw Creek people still favored the use of upland habitats to the north of the Sacramento Valley.

Around three thousand years ago, their southern boundary appears to have been contested by another group, represented by the Whiskeytown Pattern. The zone of contention was in the Sacramento River Canyon, where artifacts from both groups overlap, probably signaling a shifting territorial boundary. Anthropologists studying cultures from around the world have found that the highest degree of artistic elaboration often occurs along contested boundaries, where people seek to enhance their group identity through wearing special clothing and other creative displays; this was certainly the case among the Squaw Creek people, who wore pieces of slate engraved with detailed, abstract designs. Hundreds of these small artifacts have been recovered from a handful of Squaw Creek Pattern sites, together forming the largest portable rock art collection ever found in North America.

Although the Whiskeytown people eventually began to settle in the lowlands and increasingly relied on fishing (the latter evidenced by caches of stone net sinkers found in several of their sites), it wasn't until the arrival of the Wintu (represented by the Shasta Pattern) that full use of the salmon fishery developed. Their arrival shortly after 1500 BP was a major historical event, marked by a huge influx of people who established relatively large, permanent villages up and down the Sacramento River. Historical linguists are pretty sure the Wintu originated in Oregon and migrated southward, as their language retained words for certain plants and animals that existed only in Oregon, and it also borrowed new words for California species from local, pre-existing languages. We also know that the Wintu were actively expanding their territory in a westward direction down the Trinity River drainage based on evidence that they borrowed words for important fishing spots and mountain peaks from Chimariko populations, who were being pushed downstream at the time of historic contact.

Our excavations at SHA-1043 provided an outstanding opportunity to get a firsthand look at how the Wintu lived prior to the arrival of Europeans in the region. Careful sampling of the village deposits led to the discovery of multiple house structures, an earthen lodge, and several cooking features. We were also able to document the rich bounty of wild foods used by the Wintu, including salmon, steelhead, and small resident fishes, terrestrial game dominated by deer and elk, and a variety of plant foods including gray pine nuts, manzanita berries, and multiple kinds of acorns. The importance of these foods was also reflected by the artifacts recovered from the site, which included bone toggles from fish harpoons, flaked-stone arrow points, knives and chopping tools used to kill and butcher large game, and hopper mortars and pestles used to prepare the vegetarian side of the diet.

Multiple human burials were found along the edge of the village deposit during the early stages of our excavation, leading us to believe that we had discovered the main cemetery area of the village. Its location was consistent with old Wintu accounts, which stated that cemeteries were usually placed about one hundred yards from the houses. Based on these considerations, the burial area was preserved and no further excavations took place there. To our surprise, however, another cemetery area was found in the middle of the village, in a place that could not be avoided by the construction project. As a result, the interments were carefully removed and reburied within the original, protected cemetery area along the edge of the site.

Excavations within the new, primary cemetery area revealed a high density of individuals. Most of them were buried in the traditional way originally reported by anthropologist Cora Du Bois, with the bodies sitting in a tightly flexed position facing Mount Shasta, and placed within bark-lined pits that were covered with a combination of river cobbles and soil. Because of the regular use of this location over many years, the burial pits and stone cairns were often built on top of one another, giving the site structural characteristics similar to a mausoleum.

Interregional exchange of nonlocal commodities was evidenced by the presence of obsidian artifacts imported from adjacent areas to the north and east. Shell beads were traded in from the coast, including clamshell beads from Bodega Bay and dentalium shell from areas farther north, perhaps from as far as the Oregon coast. These items were highly valued by the Wintu, particularly the clamshell beads, which served as money. Given their high value, it is not surprising that shell beads were rarely found within the village deposits, which were dominated by refuse from day-to-day living. Shell beads *were* found in abundance, however, in burial contexts, although only in a limited number of graves. Only 25 percent of the prehistoric cemetery population possessed 90 percent of the bead wealth, clearly indicating a high degree of socioeconomic stratification within Wintu society. Such a discrepancy between the rich and poor is somewhat surprising, as many hunter-gatherer people in other parts of the world are more egalitarian in nature, with wealth and power evenly distributed across the population.

Even more surprising was the degree of violence evidenced at the site. We were first clued in to this situation by the unusual age/sex structure found within the prehistoric burial population. Most hunter-gatherer groups had relatively high degrees of infant mortality due in part to the lack of modern medicine, but after this interval most people stayed quite healthy until reaching the age of twenty. Mortality increased between ages twenty and thirty partly because female death rates were higher due to the risks associated with pregnancy and childbirth. Mortality rates then diminished to some degree during middle-age but increased again as old age set in, sometime around fifty years old. Our findings at SHA-1043 largely paralleled these trends, with one important exception: the twenty-to-thirty age interval, which should have been dominated by childbirth-related female deaths, actually had a higher frequency of male deaths—specifically deaths due to violence.

Fully 63 percent of the males between the ages of twenty and thirty had evidence of traumatic injuries to their bones. Most of these injuries were depression fractures to the skull due to clubbing; some fractures had healed, whereas others were the cause of death. Other forms of violence included death from being shot with arrows, which were often found embedded in the body. Some individuals were riddled with as many as thirty arrows, some of which featured nonlocal arrow point styles used by neighboring people. Two of these men, both in their early twenties, had been brought back to the village and buried with some of the richest grave goods observed at the site, probably indicating that they were heroic warriors highly valued by their society. These findings reveal a level of intertribal warfare far surpassing what is traditionally associated with Native California, and of a much higher intensity than reported by the Wintu interviewed by Du Bois. But given the expansionist tendencies of the Wintu—as shown by the archaeological and linguistic records—combined with the high-quality resource base along the Sacramento River, which they probably had to defend from adjacent groups living in more marginal areas, this level of violence should probably not have been so surprising after all.

Conditions got a whole lot worse when Europeans arrived in the region, bringing with them devastating diseases that Native peoples had no immunities for. Prior to these diseases, the Wintu could identify their enemies and attempt to do something about potential threats. But when John Work and his Hudson Bay Company brigade of over one hundred people entered California from the north, they brought a killer no one could see or defend themselves against.

When John Work first arrived in Wintu territory during the fall of 1832 things were relatively good. His diary reports large Indian populations in fine health and quite willing to exchange goods with him. Common items brought from Europe included glass beads and copper kettles, both of which we found within the historic-period Wintu burials at the site. These items were obviously treasured by the Wintu and easily integrated into their economic system. On his return trip during the summer of 1883, however, malaria had taken over, decimating Indian populations up and down the Central Valley.

Very few historic accounts actually document this catastrophic event, but the few we have paint a disturbing picture. According to John Work and a couple of travelers that came through the area the following year, Native people were dying so quickly that the survivors could not bury them fast enough, in some cases leaving bodies unburied across the landscape. S. F. Cook's analysis of these records in 1959 led him to conclude that at least 75 percent of the Native population may have perished as a result of the epidemic. Until now, archaeological evidence of this event has never been published.

We originally expected that the Wintu burial population from the John Work era would look quite different from the prehistoric population summarized above. If almost everyone had suddenly died from malaria, then all age groups would be evenly represented in the cemetery, along with evidence of mass burials. The latter phenomenon was definitely confirmed, as several multiperson graves were discovered and evidence showed that the traditional mode of burial was often abandoned and replaced by non-flexed interments lacking the bark-lined cairns. The age structure of the cemetery population was also significantly different, and not all age groups were affected in the same way. Not surprisingly, infant mortality remained high, but children between the ages of five and ten, who had excellent survivability in prehistoric times, were dying at a rate even higher than the infants. Death rates dropped significantly for people between ages ten and twenty, and roughly paralleled the prehistoric trends through middle-age; however, the older people tended to die about a decade sooner than was the case for the earlier, pre-contact group.

These findings indicate that the malaria epidemic hit the young and old very hard but was less devastating to those in between, particularly the teenagers. Although the burial population from SHA-1043 represents only one of many others that lay hidden in the archaeological record of Shasta County, it could indicate that Cook's mortality estimate—75 percent of the total population—was too high. There is no doubt that a major population decline occurred in the 1830s, but it is important to emphasize that enough Wintu survived to carry their cultural traditions into the 1900s, allowing the language and culture to persist into the present.

But surviving the 1830s malaria epidemic was just the first challenge set before the Wintu by the arrival of Europeans to the region. As summarized by an outstanding book entitled *Journey to Justice: The Wintu People and the Salmon* (edited by Alice R. Hoveman), the discovery of gold within the major river valleys of northern California in the 1850s brought thousands of miners to the area that had little respect for the land or the indigenous people who lived there. Indian people throughout California were driven from their lands, and in many cases killed in cold blood. Even after California achieved formal statehood in 1849, it was still legal to place orphaned Indian children into indentured servitude until the age of eighteen. Notorious characters developed an industry based on this state law, kidnapping children from remote parts of California and transporting the "orphans" to places like Sacramento for sale. Thankfully, California repealed the law in 1867 in compliance with the Fourteenth Amendment of the U.S. Constitution.

Despite this troubling history, the strength and persistence of the Wintu people insured their survival. The rich historical accounts compiled by Du Bois were collected during the 1930s, clearly showing that the culture and traditions moved forward into the modern era. But new challenges continued to arise, like the construction of Shasta Dam, which displaced many of the Winnemem Wintu and altered one of the richest salmon fisheries in the world. Many of the Wintu took jobs within the new dominant society but were still able to maintain much of their culture. Thanks to speakers of the language like Carrie Dixon, Grace McKibben, Ellen Silverthorn, and Joe Charles, a complete Wintu dictionary and other Native-language texts have been published through the University of California.

The Wintu of today are alive and well and making strong efforts to maintain many of their cultural traditions for generations to come. They belong to multiple tribal groups, including the Toyon-Wintu, the Nor-El Muk Band, the Winnemem, and the Redding Rancheria nation, the last of which has been formally recognized by the federal government, giving it the status of a sovereign nation. The Rancheria, which also includes members from adjacent tribal groups like the Yana and Pit River People, has been involved with several successful enterprises, including the management of an Indian health clinic, a Headstart program, and a grocery store; as a sovereign nation, it has also been able to develop the

Win-River Casino, which has generated a great deal of local economic development, including employment opportunities for the general public in the Redding area. Notwithstanding the time and energy required to maintain these ventures, members of the Rancheria strongly value their traditions.

Despite the lack of federal recognition, the Toyon-Wintu have also developed a variety of successful enterprises, including the Organic Production and Marketing Project, through which fruit, honey, herbs, and deer and salmon jerky produced by Native people and other organic farmers are made available at a local store. The Recycling Project, another local enterprise, repairs used computers and donates them to local nonprofit organizations, helping supply a wide range of people with needed access to technology. The Toyon-Wintu have also been involved with archaeological studies for many years, contributing to projects throughout the region. Carol Sinclair worked on the majority of these projects, teaching archaeologists like ourselves about Wintu history and many aspects of the local archaeological record she has observed over the years. Additional tribal members are becoming increasingly more involved, and Carol has passed on her knowledge to many of them. This interest was demonstrated during the current project when Gene Malone (Tribal Chairman), Kelli Hayward (Most Likely Descendant for the project), and Carol Sinclair helped with the development of our field strategy, and Carol Sinclair, Lori Light, Ester Stevenson, and Veronica Grabel participated in the actual excavations. Many of their friends and relatives visited the site on a regular basis, including non-Indian neighbors who were interested in learning about our discoveries as the project moved forward.

Native American interest in the local archaeological record is further demonstrated by the enrollment of Wintu people in classes taught at Shasta College by Eric Ritter. His course covers archaeological method and theory (including field training), providing students with a basic level of knowledge that will allow them to contribute to archaeological projects in the future. This increasing interest in archaeology is not just a local phenomenon but a movement occurring on state and national levels as well. The Society for California Archaeology has grown to more than fourteen hundred people and includes a large number of nonprofessional members. Native American participation is strong, and much of it is organized by the Society's Native American Programs Committee. Interested members of the public have also eagerly participated in the California Archaeological Site Stewardship Program, through which trained volunteers (including Native Americans) work with profession-als to protect archaeological sites by regularly visiting them and assess-ing their condition. Finally, a recent issue of the SAA *Archaeological Record* (the magazine of the Society for American Archaeology) was dedicated to "Indigenous Knowledge in Archaeological Practice," advo-cating new and innovative approaches to integrating Indian people into modern research programs.

This widespread interest in the archaeological record shouldn't be too surprising, as most people are curious about their local histories. Given that at least 95 percent of North American history occurred before the written word came to the area, much of that history can only be gleaned from the archaeological record. We have learned many things from SHA-1043, perhaps the most important being that Native cultures were far from static. Instead, they existed in a constant state of flux due to a variety of factors such as environmental change, arrival of new peoples, and invention of new technologies. During certain intervals, people lived in relative harmony with one another, but at other times they did not—this was certainly the case among the Wintu at SHA-1043. When one considers the amount of human drama encapsulated within a single place like SHA-1043, it boggles the mind how much more information must be hidden in other archaeological sites scattered across the landscape. It can't be emphasized enough that these sites are nonrenewable resources that should be protected. But if they can't be protected in whole, as was the case here, it is important that they are carefully excavated and that the findings are preserved through curation of the artifacts and through production of data-rich reports. We feel confident that we have accom-plished these goals and hope that those of you reading this book will be inspired by our efforts, perhaps leading you to learn more about prehis-tory and participate in the protection and interpretation of this valuable record that lies buried around us.

Photo Credits

**Figure 12. "Important Speakers of the Wintu Language," page 23.
University of California Press, Berkeley, California.**
Grace McKibbin: frontspiece photo in *Wintu Texts*, by Alice
Shepherd. Linguistics, vol. 117, University of California
Publications, 1989.
Carrie B. Dixon, Joe Charles, and Ellen Silverthorn: frontspiece
photos in *Wintu Grammar*, by Harvey Pitkin. Linguistics,
vol. 94, University of California Publications, 1984.

**Figure 14. "Wintu People from Birth to Middle Age," page 30.
Shasta Historical Society, SHSPhotoDatabase.**
Top Left: ID 37 Frame 71 "Baby in cradle..."
Top Right: ID 37 Frame 76 "Taken at Flatwoods..."
Bottom Left: ID 31 Frame 67 "Talitha John and Elsie Walson"
Bottom Right: ID 50 Frame 95 "Woman in buckskin..."

**Figure 15. "Wintu Elders," page 31.
Shasta Historical Society, SHSPhotoDatabase.**
Left: ID 43 Frame 38 "Millie #934 Indian Basket Weaver."
Right: ID 88 Frame 102 "Old Gunsmith."

Figure 18. "Wintu Salmon House," page 35.
National Anthropological Archives, Smithsonian Institution.
015169.00SPC "Booth for spearing salmon on the McCloud River,
c. 1880. Photography by Townsend."

Figure 20. "Salmon Drying on the River Bar," page 37.
The Bancroft Library, University of California, Berkeley.
C. Hart Merriam Collection of Native American Photographs.
1978.008 T/19a-e/3-PIC. T. WINTOON STOCK 19a-e,
Northern Wintoon Houses. ID 3 "Houses, drying racks;
McCloud River, Shasta Co.; July 1903."

Figure 29. "Traditional Wintu House Similar to Feature 3," page
55. The Bancroft Library, University of California, Berkeley.
C. Hart Merriam Collection of Native American Photographs.
1978.008 T/19a-e/2-PIC. T. WINTOON STOCK 19a-e,
Northern Wintoon Houses. ID 2 "Houses, drying racks;
McCloud River, Shasta Co.; July 1903."

Figure 33. "An Earthen Lodge from Wintoon Territory," page 59.
The Bancroft Library, University of California, Berkeley.
C. Hart Merriam Collection of Native American Photographs.
1978.008 T/19l/1-PIC. T. WINTOON STOCK 19l. Choo-hel'-
mem-sel Roundhouses. ID 1 "Roundhouses; Colusa and Glenn
Counties."

Recommended Readings

Basgall, Mark E., and William R. Hildebrandt
    1989   *Prehistory of the Sacramento River Canyon, Shasta County, California.* Center for Archaeological Research at Davis. Publication 9, University of California, Davis.

Du Bois, Cora A.
    1935   *Wintu Ethnography.* University of California Publications in American Archaeology and Ethnology 36(1):1-148.

Fagan, Brian
    2003   *Before California: An Archaeologist Looks at Our Earliest Inhabitants.* Altamira Press, New York.

Heizer, Robert F.
    1978   *California.* Edited by W. C. Sturtevant. Handbook of North American Indians, Volume 8. Smithsonian Institution, Washington, D.C.

Hoveman, Alice R.
    2002   *Journey to Justice: The Wintu People and the Salmon.* Turtle Bay Exploration Park, Redding, California.

Jones, Terry L., and Kathryn Klar
2007   *California Prehistory: Colonization, Culture, and Complexity.* Altamira Press, New York.

Maloney, Alice B.
1943   "Fur Brigade to the Bonaventura: John Work's California Expedition of 1832–1833 for the Hudson's Bay Company." *California Historical Society Quarterly* 22(3).

Sundahl, Elaine
1992   *Cultural Patterns and Chronology in the Northern California Sacramento Drainage.* Proceedings of the Society for California Archaeology 5, edited by M. D. Rosen, L. E. Christenson, and D. Laylander, pp. 89-112.

About the Authors:
Dr. William R. Hildebrandt and Michael J. Darcangelo, Far Western

Michael J. Darcangelo (left) and William R. Hildebrandt (right)

Far Western Anthropological Research Group, Inc., is a cultural resources management firm that provides consulting services in support of many state and federal environmental laws. The scope of cultural resource management is broad, incorporating prehistoric and historic archaeology, ethnography, and history, as well as contemporary Native American issues and viewpoints. For nearly thirty years, Far

Western archaeologists have conducted studies throughout California and the Great Basin, contributing to our shared understanding of the prehistoric past. But every now and then in our line of work, as *Life on the River* attests, there are insights to past peoples that emerge with startling clarity and intimacy. Far Western is proud to have been a part of this most amazing project.

Dr. William R. Hildebrandt is a principal owner of Far Western Anthropological Research Group, Inc., in Davis, California, and an adjunct professor of anthropology at the University of California, Santa Cruz. In 2001, he was appointed to the California State Historic Resources Commission by then-governor Gray Davis and served on the commission through 2005. His archaeological research has focused on hunter-gatherer adaptations in California, Oregon, and the western Great Basin. Dr. Hildebrandt is currently studying the evolution of prehistoric hunting patterns in California and the Great Basin, applying modern approaches to human behavioral ecology to this research.

Michael J. Darcangelo is a professional archaeologist who was raised in Shasta County, California. He received his B.A. in anthropology from California State University, Chico, and has worked for Far Western Anthropological Research Group, Inc., since 1994. His research interest is northern Sacramento Valley archaeology, with an emphasis on prehistoric lifeways in Shasta County.

HEYDAY INSTITUTE

Since its founding in 1974, Heyday Books has occupied a unique niche in the publishing world, specializing in books that foster an understanding of the history, literature, art, environment, social issues, and culture of California and the West. We are a 501(c)(3) nonprofit organization based in Berkeley, California, serving a wide range of people and audiences.

We are grateful for the generous funding we've received for our publications and programs during the past year from foundations and more than three hundred individual donors. Major supporters include:

Anonymous; Anthony Andreas, Jr.; Audubon California; Barnes & Noble bookstores; BayTree Fund; B.C.W. Trust III; S. D. Bechtel, Jr. Foundation; Fred & Jean Berensmeier; Book Club of California; Butler Koshland Fund; California Council for the Humanities; California State Coastal Conservancy; California State Library; Candelaria Fund; Columbia Foundation; Compton Foundation, Inc.; Malcolm Cravens Foundation; Federated Indians of Graton Rancheria; Fleishhacker Foundation; Wallace Alexander Gerbode Foundation; Marion E. Greene; Walter & Elise Haas Fund; Leanne Hinton; Hopland Band of Pomo Indians; James Irvine Foundation; George Frederick Jewett Foundation; Marty Krasney; Guy Lampard & Suzanne Badenhoop; LEF Foundation; Robert Levitt; Michael McCone; Middletown Rancheria Tribal Council; National Endowment for the Arts; National Park Service; Philanthropic Ventures Foundation; Poets & Writers; Rim of the World Interpretive Association; River Rock Casino; Riverside-Corona Resource Conservation; Alan Rosenus; San Francisco Foundation; Santa Ana Watershed Association; William Saroyan Foundation; Seaver Institute; Sandy Cold Shapero; Service Plus Credit Union; L. J. Skaggs & Mary C. Skaggs Foundation; Skirball Foundation; Orin Starn; Swinerton Family Fund; Thendara Foundation; Victorian Alliance; Tom White; Harold & Alma White Memorial Fund; and Stan Yogi.

For more information about Heyday Institute, our publications and programs, please visit our website at www.heydaybooks.com.